COMING
INTO
FOCUS

COMING INTO FOCUS

FOCUS

From an Amish Childhood to a
Journey of Many Choices

MARY KAUFMAN SCHWARTZ

TATE PUBLISHING
AND ENTERPRISES, LLC

Published by Tate Publishing & Enterprises, LLC
127 E. Trade Center Terrace | Mustang, Oklahoma 73064 USA
1.888.361.9473 | www.tatepublishing.com

Tate Publishing is committed to excellence in the publishing industry. The company reflects the philosophy established by the founders, based on Psalm 68:11,
"The Lord gave the word and great was the company of those who published it."

Book design copyright © 2012 by Tate Publishing, LLC. All rights reserved.
Cover design by Kristen Verser
Interior design by Sarah Kirchen
Author Photo by Deborah Barry

Published in the United States of America

ISBN: 978-1-61862-078-1
1. Biography & Autobiography / Personal Memoirs
2. Biography & Autobiography / Cultural Heritage
12.04.30

FOR MY SON:

Charles Christopher Stein

&

FOR MY GRANDDAUGHTERS:

Madeleine Ruth McKinney
Chloe Michelle Callander
Sophia Elaine Stein
Audrey Marie Stein
Lindsay Alane Gilpin

ACKNOWLEDGMENTS

I am deeply grateful to the many people who have supported me in the process of writing *Coming Into Focus*.

My sister and brother-in-law, Fran and Bob Gerber, as well as my brother and sister-in-law, Sam and Joan Kaufman, kept asking me, "When are you going to publish your book?" It helped to know that they supported me in publishing.

The first people other than my family that I read my stories to were the members of my Talking Circle. Their encouragement and support helped me feel as if my stories were worth hearing from people outside of my family.

My creativity group and women's group, Barbara Bellassai, Linda Gannon, and Tari Riley gave me ever-ready support and a repeated shove to continue when I got bogged down. Linda and I also met weekly for months, encouraging each other in our writing.

My niece, Deb Barry, was gracious and extremely helpful in numerous ways, and especially in putting the photos in their proper form for publication.

I asked Frances Baker to keep my feet to the fire until I got a publisher for my manuscript. She did!

I appreciate Jackie Wyse's kindness in gently prodding me to bring clarity to my sentences. Colleen Murphy's excitement about my writing, her over all guidance in my "book project," her editing, and her encouragement to publish helped me to push on.

Amy Gingerich reviewed my manuscript, and made excellent suggestions to improve the flow of my stories.

I am grateful to Hillary Atkinson, my Tate Publishing conceptual editor, for her kind and expert assistance in making the final edits to my manuscript.

If it had not been for my desire to have my son, Christopher, know his family history, I probably would not have completed writing my stories.

Most of all, I am grateful to my husband, Larry. He delighted in many of my stories, provided the security I needed to look at the painful ones, and nudged me to finish my manuscript. Without him, this book would not have happened.

TABLE OF

CONTENTS

Some names and places have been changed
in order to provide for anonymity.

INTRODUCTION

I often wonder how a young Amish girl roaming the fields on a farm in Ohio became a woman who lived in Europe, gave birth to a non-Amish son, divorced, became a psychologist, and married a wonderful Jewish man. My life has encompassed an incredible amount of richness, several periods of intense pain, and immense change. Sometimes I couldn't seem to catch up with myself. My life changed so fast that I didn't feel solid inside.

My purpose in writing these stories is to make sense of the fragments of my life that I couldn't seem to fit into place. As I started to write, I found the thoughts that came to me were the happy times of childhood, the wonderful memories I hold close to my heart. It was only after I clearly remembered those that I was able to focus on the painful memories of transition. It became clearer that I needed the happy memories as a base in order to cushion the painful ones. As I wrote, I found myself able to face parts of me I had avoided for a long time. I continue with that process.

My second reason for writing these stories is to record a history of my transition and an account of our family for my son, Christopher. I want to give him and his daughters, Sophia and Audrey, a record of their heritage so they will know where they came from. I hope it will help guide them on their way.

As I proceeded with my writing and began to envision compiling it into a book, a third purpose emerged. I hope this book will help people more clearly understand the pain and triumph of transitions so they can be increasingly sensitive to themselves and others who are making major changes, and, in particular, cultural changes.

What follows is my story so far. It has been healing and humbling for me to write it. I hope reading it will encourage other people to write their stories for themselves and their families.

MY SPECIAL LUNCH

Every morning my mamm packs a wonderful hot dog sandwich for my school lunch. I smell it cooking when I'm eating my breakfast—the salty smell of a hot dog cooking on the stove. I help her watch to make sure it's big enough—that means it's done, but not too big—that means it's tough. When it is one and a half times the size it was before it was cooked, that's when it's done. Then my mother takes a fork and takes it out and puts in on a small plate. She slits it the long way right down the middle, almost all the way through. She cuts just enough that it can lie flat. Then she puts it on one side of a piece of whole wheat bread, puts a little bit of mustard on top, and folds it over. And my sandwich is made! She wraps it in wax paper and puts it in my lunch box, along with maybe a carrot, an apple or canned peaches, and a piece of cake. I put milk into my thermos, add Hershey's chocolate syrup to it, and stir it up with a spoon.

I love my hot dog sandwich. By the time lunch comes around, the bread is just a little bit wet around the middle and the hot dog is cold, and I can't wait to bite into it. The sharp taste of the mustard. The cold taste of the hot dog. No one else at my school ever has a hot dog for lunch.

You want to know why I like hot dogs so much? Well, you're never going to see a field of hot dogs growing on a farm. We grow corn and wheat and hay. And we milk cows—but we don't grow hot dogs.

And when I eat hot dogs, I feel sort of special. And I don't feel Amish and different. Because hot dogs are like everybody else. The other day when I was walking to school, the yellow bus from the town school went past, and the kids all just looked at me. Nobody smiled or waved or nothing. They just looked. And I felt bad. That happens a lot —people just look—and it makes me feel real bad. It's because we look different.

But when I eat my hot dog sandwich, I don't feel different. I feel like everybody else. Every time.

CHILDHOOD

As a child, my life revolved around family, work, and roaming the fields. It was a happy time.

An Unknown Word

I didn't know what a scarf was. My friend Robert had excitedly asked me to get my scarf so we could play a game. I wanted to get whatever it was he wanted, but I didn't know what he was talking about. I was embarrassed. I didn't want to tell him I didn't know what a scarf was, but what else could I do? So I told him. Robert then explained to me that a scarf was the green cloth I wore on my head when I came to school, and it was hanging with my coat in the vestibule. I ran and grabbed it, and we played our game.

Robert didn't seem disturbed by my lack of knowledge, but it upset me. I didn't want to be different; I didn't want to be ignorant of English words, which seemed so natural for him to know. Robert, my teacher's son, was in the first grade with me. He was the only child in my school who was not from the neighborhood and one of the very few who weren't Amish. I liked playing with him because he was different from us. I learned new things from him. He was my special friend.

Among other things, being friends with Robert expanded my vocabulary. But the lessons were not always easy. The day I learned the meaning of scarf was the first time I remember being embarrassed because

I didn't know the words and ways of the non-Amish culture around me.

From Robert I learned that scarf meant *kopduch*. Today there are still English words I have difficulty remembering. I keep forgetting the word for *kandel*. Or *pannedreya*. These are ordinary words but words I don't read about in books or use as I talk with my friends. *Pannedreya* seems a much better word than spatula. And as for *kandel*, I still can't remember what to call the troughs at the edge of house roofs.

The Saturday Night Ritual

During my childhood, Saturday night was bathing and hair-braiding time. For the entire family, becoming clean and neat was part of preparing ourselves for Sunday. It was the last thing we did before going to bed.

"Get ready to do your hair," my mother said as she finished wiping off the kitchen counter. I did what she asked. First, I quickly unbraided my long, thick, dark brown hair. As my hair loosened, I moved my fingers through its wavy strands, working out a tangle here and there. With my braids completely unraveled, my head felt free and unencumbered. I looked at my hair as it rested on my shoulders and admired the waves resulting from the tight braids I had worn all week.

I mused about what it would be like to wear my hair down all the time, like the English. Then I slowly arched my neck backwards while pulling the ends of my hair as far down my buttocks as possible. I liked that my hair was so long I could sit on its very edge. I smiled as I moved my fingers again through the soft waves where the plaits had been and then hurried to the hand-washing sink next to the kitchen to search for a comb. A slender black one awaited me on the sink's counter, and I carried it to the dining room. Then I pushed a chair as close as possible to the circle of dim light radiating from the kerosene lamp on the dining room table. When all these tasks were completed, I sat down, and Mother placed a basin of water on the table and began combing my hair.

As she worked, my mother periodically dipped the comb into the water. The wet comb dampened my long strands of hair, helping to secure each one in place. It hurt when my mother coaxed the tangles out; every time I tensed my shoulders. Getting rid of the tangles only took a minute, but it seemed much longer. After my hair was fully combed out, Mother made a part down the middle of my head, grasped a front quarter of hair, and began braiding.

She pulled the strands of hair so tight I felt as if tiny pin pricks were exploding on my head. She pulled so hard I knew my eyes must look Asian.

"It hurts," I complained as I hunched over the edge of the chair.

"You will be finished soon," Mother said as she continued braiding.

Every hair needed to be wet down and in place. The next day was Sunday, and I needed to look neat.

After my mother had finished braiding that first quarter of hair, she divided the corresponding back quarter into two strands. With the two strands and the already completed plait, she began to form a larger braid. Half of my hair continued to hang loose.

As my mother braided, we talked. I can't remember about what. Often my sisters sat nearby and joined in the conversation. It was the one time during the week that focused mainly on me. It was a special half hour.

When my mother had almost finished the large braid, she carefully inserted into one of the strands a piece of thin white string, which had previously been unraveled from the seam of a feed sack. Then she continued plaiting to the end, wrapped the string around the bottom of the braid and quickly knotted it.

Mother continued the same pattern of braiding with the remainder of my loose hair. When the second large braid was completed, she began wrapping both braids around the lower back of my head, slipping the ends (and the two strings) underneath the first, smaller braids from the front quarters of hair. She pulled the strings tightly until the larger braids fit smoothly around my head. Then she tied the strings together to keep my braids secure so my church cap would fit properly. After that she bound a long, white organdy scarf on my head so that not one hair would be out of place in the morning.

"There, you're done!" she announced.

I felt warm inside going to bed, knowing that my hair had been braided for the week, that I was clean and ready for Sunday, and knowing that things were orderly and in place.

My Black Velvet Mandly

When I was a little girl, I had a beautiful cape, which we called a *mandly*. It was black velvet—intense black and soft. Each time as I was putting it on, I would pause to gently stroke it with my hand. At the top my *mandly* closed with several large black buttons, and it was so long that it extended almost to the bottom of my calf-length dress. It kept me very warm.

I don't know where my *mandly* came from. It was not a hand-me-down from my sisters, like most of my other clothes. From the softness in my mother's eyes and the smile on her lips, I could tell my *mandly* was special to her, although she never said so, and she never explained why.

I owned no article of clothing that was unique except for my *mandly*. All Amish people wore clothes made from the same basic patterns. The only distinguishing features were a tuck here or a hemline there. Women embroidered their initials into their bonnets, coats, and shawls in order to tell them apart.

But my *mandly* needed no initials. It was black velvet instead of woolen and soft as rabbit's fur. I stood taller and straighter and held my head higher whenever I wore it.

Maybe my *mandly* is where my love of beautiful clothes began.

From Sacks to Underwear

I sat on the grass and watched a tall man in beige pants carry sacks of feed into the dark belly of our barn. The white cotton bags were imprinted with advertising slogans and designs. I knew that my underpants and slips would be made from these sacks.

When the sacks were empty, my mother would ask me or one of my sisters to undo the seams. It was a trick to find the end of the lone thread used to sew the sides of the fabric together and then to slip that end through a loop the thread formed right below. When I finally accomplished these tasks, I swiftly pulled the thread as far as my short arm could reach, two or three times in a row. This process took less than a minute, quickly resulting in an open seam. I relished the wonderful freedom of ripping the seam apart. As I worked, a slight dust from the remnants of feed in the bags radiated around me, accompanied by a musty odor. After I had finished, my mother would wash and bleach the sacks, cut the fabric, and sew underpants and slips for the women in our family.

I didn't like wearing those undergarments when they were new, because the fabric was thick and scratchy. However, after a few washings, my slips and underpants felt soft and comfortable.

Sometimes, the bleach Mother used didn't remove quite all the color on the feed sacks, and the words and designs printed on the fabric were still faintly visible. I liked that. It was the only time I was permitted to wear anything multicolored. And no one could see it—it was a secret.

Recently, my sister told me the words *Full of Pep* were printed on some of the bags. She said our mother always made sure she didn't use that part of the sack to make our underpants!

A Dangerous Dive

My first and only dive was onto our straw stack.

I had read about swimming in library books. In magazines, I had seen glamorous young women in red bathing suits gracefully diving. But I had never observed anyone swim, and the idea of being water-bound fascinated me. Diving seemed especially wonderful and free, almost like flying, and I wanted to do it. I was about eight years old.

I thought about swimming for a long time. We didn't have a swimming pool. We didn't have swim suits, and we didn't go swimming. There was a pond on our farm. We walked by it, and the cattle sometimes drank water from it, but no one ever swam in it. I never even considered swimming there, because I was certain I would drown. Eventually, I decided to dive from the open door of the second floor of the barn onto the straw stack below.

I chose a day when no one was in the barn and stood at the edge of the open door for a long time. I stretched up my arms and stood some more. The straw stack seemed a long way off, and I knew I had to push hard in order to land on the straw and not on the ground. Slowly and gracefully I dove off, head first, with outstretched arms. My body felt weightless. The straw approached swiftly.

It was not a smooth landing.

The rough straw scratched the skin on my hands, face, and forehead—tiny beads of blood appeared like miniature red poppies in a distant field. My skin smarted, my head hurt, and my neck felt disjointed. All of me ached. I was stunned.

I sat on the straw stack for a long time. Slowly the world quit spinning, and my body ceased throbbing. I told no one.

That afternoon, I learned that straw stacks were not meant for diving. Even today, when I step into a swimming pool, a bit of fear from my initial dive returns, and I do not feel safe.

To Town with My Father

When I was a little girl I loved going to town with my father in the summer. (In the winter I couldn't go with him, because he usually went during the middle of the week when I was in school.) About once a week, I overheard my father mention something about going to town to run some errands.

I always eagerly asked, "May I go?"

He almost always said yes. I then hurried to my mother and told her my father had said I could go.

Her smiling brown eyes looked into mine as she said, "Well, then you need to get ready."

I found a comb, wet it, and tried to comb back the hairs that had escaped my braids. (There were always a few rebellious strands that refused to comply.) If I needed help, my mother would help me. Then I washed my bare feet and changed my clothes, donning a clean apron or dress, my shoes, and my black bonnet. Finally, I was ready.

By then my father had hitched our horse, Homer, to the buggy, and we were off.

It was pleasant driving the three miles to the general store as the horse's hooves clip-clopped down the road. The countryside was intensely green, serene, and beautiful. My father and I didn't talk much; I was quietly anticipating the excitement of being in town. We passed neighbors and friends along the way. My father waved and said, "Ha du" to everyone we saw, because it was the courteous thing to do.

When we arrived in town, I asked my father if I could have a little bit of money. He always said yes, giving me a nickel or a dime. While my father filled my mother's grocery list, I went to the candy counter to ponder what I wanted to buy.

I always stood in front of the glass counter and admired the goodies for a while. Arranged in rows on two shelves were small open boxes of bubble gum and regular gum, candy cigarettes and life savers, lollipops of all flavors (which we called suckers), fireballs, candy bars, and tootsie rolls. I seldom chose a candy bar, because it cost five cents, and once I opened it, I couldn't keep from eating it all at once. Plus, such a purchase would leave little or no money for buying anything else.

After I had gazed at the goodies for a few minutes, the kindly middle-aged female clerk asked, "May I help you?"

Piece by piece, I told her what I wanted. She put the candies and gum in a small brown paper bag, which she handed to me as I gave her my coin.

When my father had finished making his purchases, we crawled back into the buggy and drove home. Later, I sat on the lawn and carefully laid out my treasures. My mouth watered as I anticipated the flavor, density, and sweetness of each. I remember the candy cigarettes the most fondly. They were white with pink tips and came in a box resembling a real pack of cigarettes.

I loved sitting on the lawn, sometimes wearing my red cowboy hat, "smoking" my cigarettes. I felt a bit wicked, as if I belonged to a foreign world where all things were possible.

A Promise to My Mother

I meandered into the dining room one morning and found my mother sitting in a chair by the corner weeping. I was frightened. I had never seen Mother cry before. And I had seldom seen her sitting down during the midmorning of a weekday. Usually she was busy cooking, cleaning, doing laundry, or sewing. I hurried to her, put my hands in her lap, and asked, "What is the matter, Mamm?"

Through her tears my mother implored, "Promise me you will never leave the Amish?"

I couldn't bear to see my mother cry. Slowly my lips parted. I took a deep breath. Looking at the floor, I softly told her, "I'll stay Amish, Mamm."

In the next few minutes, the tears flowing from my mother's eyes gradually lessened, though she continued wiping her eyes with her white handkerchief. I slowly tiptoed out of the dining room and into the living room. There I sat cross-legged on the sofa, staring into space. My heart ached for my mother. But I dreamed of a life where I would travel to faraway places, wear beautiful clothes, and go away to college like my sister Alma. I was certain I did not want to stay Amish. I couldn't have been more than eight years old.

About fifteen minutes earlier, Alma had left to return to Goshen College. During her visit home, it had become clear to my mother that Alma would never live as an Amish person again. Alma was thrilled about being in college—she delighted in her history classes, she savored her friendships with students from other countries, and she enjoyed wearing non-Amish clothes. The sparkle in Alma's eyes and the lilt in her voice were never greater than when she was telling us about her new life.

All of my siblings had either taken steps to leave the Amish or were thinking of doing so. My brother Leo no longer wore Amish clothes or went to the Amish church. Sarah was thinking of taking the GED, as Alma had done, and also was contemplating attending the Mennonite church. Allen was exploring Pax, an alternative for military service. If he joined, he would be going to Europe. Fannie and Ada both planned to go to high school and eventually become members of the Mennonite church as well. And even Sam, who was only ten years old, already knew he wanted to attend high school. I was Mother's last hope.

Because I had made a promise to my mother, I tried hard to imagine staying Amish for the rest of my life. I envisioned remaining home while my brothers and sisters went to college. I pictured myself marrying an Amish boy and living on a farm. Canning, cooking, cleaning, and raising many children would fill my days while my siblings roamed the world. I felt as if I were wearing shackles. It was not many months before I again knew that I would leave the Amish and that I could not keep the promise I had made to my mother.

My mother's grief saddened me, because her dreams for me were not my dreams. I never told her I couldn't keep my promise.

Quarantined from Church

I leaned toward my mother and asked permission to go to the bathroom. She nodded, so I tiptoed past rows of women trying to make themselves comfortable, hunched over on backless wooden benches, their children snuggled against them. After finishing in the bathroom, I walked to a table nearby. I grasped a small handful of pretzels from a glass bowl with one hand and a sour cream cookie from a china plate with the other. My mouth watered. Then I hurried back to the bench where my mother was sitting and slid into my seat. After swiftly taking a bite from the cookie, I saw, to my dismay, that I had already consumed a large portion of my treat. To make it last longer, I began taking small bites. It was wonderful to savor the sweetness— to do something other than sit silently, listening to the droning of the preacher and observing the people around me. I had already been doing that for more than an hour, and it would be at least another hour and a half before church was over.

As I ate, a few cookie crumbs fell on the white organdy apron covering the length of my Sunday dress. I loved wearing my best dress, crisp apron, and patent leather shoes. Because church was held every other Sunday, I could only wear them once every two weeks. My eyes wandered around the crowded dining room, one of four or five rooms transformed into the space for today's church service. Located on the main floor of the house, these rooms were overflowing with people. The preacher stood sideways in the doorway, which separated the living room and the dining room, his back nearly touching the frame. His shoulders slightly bent, he turned to direct his words first to the congregants in the living room. After a few minutes, he rotated his body to face those of us in the dining room. The people seated in the more distant rooms could hear the preacher but not see him.

I liked it best when we had church in a barn rather than in a house. A barn's second floor was more spacious than any of our houses. In a barn everyone in the congregation could see everyone else, including the preacher, and more fresh air circulated in barns than in houses. But that day, church was meeting at a neighbor's house, because it was winter and our barns would have been too cold.

I was very excited when it was announced at the end of the service that the next church meeting would be held at our home.

When I was about nine years old, I got the measles at the worst possible time: the night before we were having church at our house. All week long I had been looking forward to Sunday, imagining so many of my friends and neighbors coming to visit all at once. Church was the only occasion throughout the year when more than one or two families were invited to our house on the same day. After school and in the evenings, I energetically helped my mother by washing dishes, sweeping the floor, and completing other tasks she assigned to me.

On Saturday evening everything was ready for church. The house was thoroughly cleaned with the help of neighbors, sour cream cookies were made, and pretzels were bought. Throughout the first floor our furniture was pushed back along the walls, and backless benches were placed in rows in the kitchen, living room, dining room, and hallway. Outside, the yard and barnyard were in order. And for the after-church lunch, my mother and sisters had prepared Swiss cheese, sweet pickles, sliced boloney, red beets, cracked wheat and white breads, apple butter, and a wonderful marshmallow peanut butter spread.

Because of all the excitement, I knew I would have difficulty sleeping that night. But I didn't know there would be another reason why sleep might elude me. When it became dark and my whole family was almost ready for bed, I began feeling sick. My throat hurt, my forehead burned, and I felt unusually tired. I told my mother.

Her eyes searched mine for signs of illness, while her cool hands touched my sore throat and my hot forehead. She noted a few spots on my cheeks and murmured, "Why, I think you have the measles."

"The measles!" I exclaimed in disbelief. "I don't want to have the measles." I felt a sudden heaviness in my chest as my mind flooded with all I would miss if I was sick: experiencing our house full of people, talking and playing with my friends after church, sitting at long tables formed from church benches where we would eat boloney, Swiss cheese, and bread with peanut butter spread.

My mother said, "Go to bed, and we'll see how you are in the morning."

The next morning I felt worse, but I hoped I was still well enough to be in church. The glands in my throat were larger than ever, and the spots on my face had multiplied.

My mother declared, "You do have the measles."

I felt numb inside.

Signs saying "Measles, Stay Out" were posted on the doors to my sisters' bedroom, where I was to stay during church. Centrally located, their second-floor room faced the front yard, offering a better view of the driveway and yard than the room did that I shared with my sister Sarah.

I felt depressed and alone as I sat on the floor, glued to the window of my sisters' bedroom. I could see a lot. Buggies rolled down the road and into our driveway. Familiar faces crawled out of the buggies; their clothes were nearly identical. Everyone was dressed in his or her Sunday best. Black shawls and bonnets, black shoes and stockings, plain-colored dresses and white aprons for the married women. Plain-colored dresses and matching aprons for the single women. Black *mandlys* (capes) covering white aprons and plain-colored dresses for the little girls. Black hats and suits over white shirts for the men. One after another they arrived. The women and children hurried into the house, while the men unhitched the horses and led them into the barn.

People entered the house quietly. For about twenty minutes, I heard nothing more than periodic soft-spoken voices and later only a child's occasional cry. When the solemn medieval-sounding chants of Amish singing began, I knew that church was starting. The lead singer's high-pitched male voice led the first part of each verse and was then joined by the congregation's mixed voices, singing in unison. The beauty of the singing filled me with reverence and awe.

Then the sermons and prayers began, and they went on for hours. I felt increasingly bored and alone. I was sad that I couldn't be with everyone else downstairs. I peered out the window, but no one was visible except an occasional man walking toward the barn to relieve himself and then back into the house. (Only women and children used the bathroom inside.) Below, the lone sound of a preacher's voice droned on and on.

Suddenly I heard soft footsteps coming up the stairs. I listened. The door opened, and my father stepped in. In his hand was a small white plate holding two cookies! I was amazed, because my father had never brought me cookies before. My mother and sisters took care of me; my father worked in the fields and barn.

My father smiled as he handed the plate of cookies to me and quietly asked, "Are you all right?"

I told him I was. In our family it was not acceptable to complain to him. Because my father was a bit shy, I knew he must care about me very much if he had walked up the open stairway with rows of people sitting nearby to bring me something special. I felt less alone.

Around noon church was over. The sound of voices increased downstairs. When I smelled coffee brewing, I knew lunch was being prepared. I tried to imagine what was happening below by remembering my participation in past church days, by listening to the sounds of clinking teacups and chatting voices and by glancing out the window at the men standing around outside, talking in small groups. In the middle of the afternoon, a teenage boy wandered into my room in spite of the signs posted on the door. He looked surprised when he found me there, said hello, and ambled out. I hardly knew him and was glad when he left. A bit later I heard several teenage girls giggling and chatting outside the door, and then they walked in. They also seemed startled to see me, said hello, and went back out.

Later in the afternoon, my sisters stopped by, one by one. I was delighted to see them.

First Fannie came. She asked, "Are you all right?"

A bit later the door opened and Ada walked in. She grinned at me and asked, "How are the measles?"

Still later Sarah came and inquired, "Do you need anything?"

No one stayed long, because each was busy helping to prepare lunch and then cleaning up afterward. I felt lonelier than ever after they all had left.

At nearly five o'clock, Sarah came into the room again. She smiled and said, "Almost everyone has gone. I think it's all right for you to come downstairs now."

I quickly exited the bedroom and walked into the hallway, breathing fast. As I descended the stairs, I inhaled the pungent odor of coffee and the lingering scent of many people. The furniture was still pushed against the walls, as it had been when I went upstairs in the morning. A few wooden backless benches remained in the living room, where several women sat in a group chatting softly. At the other end of the room, three or four men were sitting and talking, their legs outstretched, their bodies leaning against the backs of their chairs. I quickly scanned each room, taking in as much of what had happened as I could. The empty benches and used coffee cups testified to the people who had come and gone.

Later in the evening, I lay crosswise on a double bed with my sisters and several of their friends. We giggled as they told funny stories. I was the youngest and mostly listened. No one acted afraid of getting the measles from me. I felt wonderful and warm inside and was delighted to be in the midst of my family again.

The Too-Fancy Dress

My father's irate shout pierced the afternoon stillness. I dropped my grass-trimming shears, jerked my head toward his voice, and held my breath.

Dad screamed from fifty feet away, "No daughter of mine is going to wear a dress like that."

My sister Ada, clothed in her new pale yellow dress, was standing in the yard a short distance from my father. She looked beautiful and graceful in the dress's fitted bodice and slightly gathered skirt. Her dark brown hair gleamed from the light of the sun. Ada was a freshman in high school.

My father was angry because the dress was multicolored—a field of embroidered white daisies bedecked the yellow bodice. The dress was one of Ada's first non-Amish garments.

I ached inside from my father's outburst. I wished he could be happy instead of worried and angry. I wished he was excited about the lifestyle he saw my siblings and me choosing. I wished he enjoyed the dress's beauty. I was about eleven years old and savored dreaming about the clothes I would wear someday—gorgeously colored dresses, skirts, and blouses made from creative patterns like my sister's.

Ada kept the yellow dress. For a while she wore it only when she was out of my father's sight. I don't remember anyone in my family ever mentioning the dress again.

Thrashing Day

I encircled a pile of wheat kernels with my arms opened wide and pulled them toward me again and again. It was dusty and hot in the granary on the second floor of our barn. Chaff permeated the air as streams of wheat steadily sputtered from the tin tube protruding through the window to my left. The tube was an arm of the thrashing machine, which was positioned just outside the granary window on the barn floor. To my right, my father was on his knees in the grain, shoveling the kernels toward the edges of the small wooden room. We worked continuously and swiftly so the wheat wouldn't pile up and bury the tube.

When one part of the granary was piled high, my father would shift the tube to another area of the room. By mid-afternoon the kernels would be heaped up three-quarters of the way to the ceiling, and I would begin to feel closed in. Because two people could no longer fit in the granary, I would leave in order to avoid being buried in the grain. My father would exit in the late afternoon, when the grain was too high for him to shovel anymore. By evening, when I would be relaxing on the lawn or completing a few tasks for my mother, the grain would finally reach near the top of the low-ceilinged room. But for now, I kept on handling the grain, accompanied by the pounding of the thrashing machine motor thundering like a freight train passing overhead.

Outside the granary on the barn floor, bearded men in straw hats, blue denim pants, and short-sleeved shirts labored on a wagon next to the thrashing machine. They were busily feeding sheaves of wheat into the huge, gray metal machine nearby. The size of a semi, it shook as it worked. The large draft horses hitched to the wagon twitched, swishing their tails to shoo away the pesky flies.

Bright sunlight shone through a large open doorway on the south side of the barn. A thrashing machine pipe spewed straw through the doorway. The straw shot up into the air and landed on the ground outside. A man on top of the machine maneuvered the tube so the straw would pile up, forming a round stack. The mound would be taller than the ceiling of the first floor of the barn before the day was finished. The straw would be used to bed animals in the barn in the winter.

Earlier in the day, I had been very disappointed when my mother said that I was too old to be out with the men. I was eleven or twelve years old and near puberty. But when the wheat started spouting into the granary and my father had trouble keeping up with the shoveling by himself, he sent for me in spite of my age. I ran to the barn, joyous that I could help after all. I loved being in the granary with my father and outside working with the thrashers. It was infinitely more interesting than being in the house and cooking for the men's noon dinner.

Halfway through the morning, two of my sisters appeared carrying glass gallon jars, one full of water, the other of lemonade. Water had condensed on the outside of the jars, and triangles of lemon floated on the surface of the lemonade. My sisters filled glasses with the refreshments and handed them to the men. I was pleased to be handed a glass also. It signified that I was one of the laborers. I tried to drink my glass of lemonade quickly in order to get back to work as soon as possible. Normally I liked to sip on my lemonade, but because I was with the men, I didn't allow myself to. I loved the sweet liquid, the tanginess of lemons, the way it quenched my thirst. I gulped it down as fast as I could.

We worked until noon. By then my mother and sisters had cooked a huge meal to feed the hungry thrashers. All the men strolled toward the house, taking off their straw hats as they neared it. Buckets and basins filled with water, along with cakes of white soap were resting on a bench in our front yard. Once the men reached the benches, they took turns washing their arms, hands, and faces. Then they filed into the kitchen, which was filled with the aroma of good cooking and on into the dining room, where they sat at a long table loaded with food. The meal included bowls of mashed potatoes topped with trickles of brown melted butter, pan-fried chicken, roast beef, gravy, applesauce, pickles and red beets, coleslaw, lettuce salad, fresh vegetables from the garden, bread with butter, jam and apple butter, cherry pies, a white cake, coffee, and tea.

I did not eat with the men. Even though I had helped with the thrashing, it was unthinkable for a girl or woman to sit at the table with the thrashers. If there had been room, it would have been all right for my brother to eat there, but not for me. I knew this and accepted it, but I didn't like it. I didn't waste time thinking about it for long. The women ate when the men were finished.

Soon after the men entered the house, I grinned at my brother and whispered wryly, "Let's move their hats."

His eyes sparkled, and he nodded in agreement. We giggled softly as we stealthily removed each hat from the tree branch or porch railing where its owner had carefully placed it, and then mixed them up.

After Sam and I had successfully completed our plot, we waited outside while my mother and sisters finished serving the men in the dining room. We lay on the grass in the yard, resting and entertaining ourselves. Through the open doors we could hear some of what was going on inside. And besides, I had observed enough thrashers' meals to be able to picture the scene in my mind perfectly. The meal began and ended with a silent prayer, as was customary in Amish homes. The men piled their plates full. Throughout the meal, brief, quiet bits of conversation filtered out of the room, as did the clinking of metal utensils on china. Now and then someone joked a bit. Dishes were soon empty, but then desserts were passed by my sisters, and the same plates were again filled.

When the men appeared from the house to retrieve their hats, quiet confusion emerged. The hats were so similar that it was hard to distinguish one from another. The men appeared disgruntled, and none of them smiled. Sam and I sat on the grass some distance away, glanced at each other, and grinned. Pretending not to notice the thrashers, we snuck glimpses of them picking up and examining one hat after another until each found his own.

After dinner, the men again went to the barn and fields to continue their work. My brother and I quickly filled our plates, gulped our food, and hurried out to help—I to the barn and he to the fields. In the middle of the afternoon, the men gathered on the lawn for pints of vanilla, chocolate, and strawberry ice cream, which one of my sisters had brought from town. (We didn't own a freezer, since we had no electricity.) My brother and I were also given ice cream. We sat a bit apart from the men under a shade tree. With each bite, my tongue lingered over the smooth strawberry flavor.

Occasionally, thrashing took a day and a half rather than only a day. But regardless of how long it took, by the time thrashing was finished, the granary was full and our straw stack was high. As always, we smiled with satisfaction when our work was successfully completed for the season. I felt tired and gratified.

Later that evening we watched the thrashing machine slowly roll out of our lane, pulled by a metal-wheeled tractor driven by a neighbor. The thrashing machine and tractor were then delivered to the next farm. Each farmer in the neighborhood helped the other farmers with their thrashing. If the farmer himself couldn't go, he would send a grown son or hired hand to assist. The work continued until each family's wheat had been harvested for the season.

The Story

I remember the excitement I felt in my eighth-grade one-room country school as I responded to my friend Sarah's statement, "I bet you are going on to high school." A few classmates sat listening to our conversation.

I proudly said, "Yes, I am going. I can't wait. I want to get out of here and do things."

My schoolmates looked away from me and said nothing. None of them were going to high school or "getting out of here." I don't know that any of them wanted to.

Slowly, the word must have spread. Schoolmates who used to be my friends no longer talked to me much, nor did they seem interested in what I had to say. One day during recess, several boys began taunting a bright girl whose family was poor and not well-respected in the community. I made a statement defending her, but they kept on demeaning her as if I had said nothing. It was then that I knew my power to influence my classmates was gone.

Several weeks later, while I was going to the bathroom during the noon recess, I learned just how much my position with my schoolmates had changed. The small, windowless outhouse smelled faintly of urine. It was musty from the damp weather. Because I wasn't wearing a jacket, I felt chilly and was eager to hurry back into the schoolhouse as fast as I could. I quickly sat down on one of the two wooden toilet seats. Suddenly the door burst open.

Three boys my age, who had formerly been my friends, stood outside and peered in. Two of them had "liked me" in the past. The boys were bigger than I was, and they glared at me as the brisk wind blew their hair wildly. Then they laughed, walked back and forth in front of the john, and taunted me. One carried a big stick. I sat immobilized with my underpants down. They paced back and forth for three or four minutes, laughing and threatening me. And then, abruptly, they left. The door stood wide open. No one was in sight.

I stood, pulled up my underpants, and ran inside the one-room schoolhouse, where there was safety in numbers. It was warm, and the students were quieting down, as always happened when recess was ending. I went to my desk on the right side of the room where the seats for the eighth graders were and hurriedly sat down. The familiar room didn't seem quite real.

I didn't tell our teacher, Mr. Rank, about the harassment. He had made a few feeble efforts during the early part of the school year to discipline the older boys, but they laughed at him and left the building whenever they wanted to. He no longer tried to stop them from misbehaving.

As soon as I arrived home from school that afternoon, I told my parents and sisters what had happened. I was so horrified that I could not remember what the boys had said as they taunted me.

I insisted, "I'm not going back."

My parents were tight lipped and said little.

My sisters' faces were grim with anger as they agreed, "No, you are not going back. You can go to school at Berlin."

Berlin was one of the town schools where parents in neighboring communities sent their children in order to avoid one-room schools.

Later that evening my mother and father went into their bedroom and shut the door. When my mother came out ten minutes later, her face was dark. She reluctantly told me, "I guess you can go to Berlin."

Before hearing about the harassment from my classmates, my parents would not have considered letting me go to school anywhere but Leeper until I completed the eighth grade. Berlin was fifteen miles away, and few Amish students went to school there.

I was both scared and excited the next morning. I had planned to go to Berlin High in the fall, but I was now able to attend the town school months earlier. I drove to Berlin with Fran (Fannie started to identify herself as Fran before going to high school), Ada, and Sam. My sisters and I stopped at the office and told the secretary I had come to enroll, and then we found the eighth-grade classroom together. It was located in the same building as my siblings' classrooms.

I felt shy as I entered the brightly lit room. Everyone quieted down and stared at me. My chest tightened, and I felt my face flush. The students looked different than the ones at Leeper. They all seemed to be the same age, many were wearing brightly colored, fashionable clothes, and some wore multi-colors. The girls had styled and cut their hair in a great variety of ways, and only a few had caps on their heads. The boys wore short hair, and most had flat tops. I had met only a few students in the class before: my cousin Gladys and several boys and girls from summer Bible school at the Mennonite church my sisters and brothers attended.

The teacher looked around the room and quickly said, "We have no desk for you."

I don't remember how it happened, but I ended up sharing a desk with my cousin, for which I was grateful. I felt strange and uncomfortable but exhilarated.

All day long we had classes. It was not like my little one-room school, where Mr. Rank merely made an attempt at teaching. He eyed the back wall when he talked, he spoke half-heartedly, and he taught classes only part of the day. Also I was excited to notice library books on many students' desks. At Leeper the only books in the building were our texts, plus about twenty books delivered each month in a white drawstring sack from the county library. I loved reading and quickly devoured almost every library book—except the science books. I didn't care if some of the books were geared to grades much lower than mine. They all contained something new and interesting.

But I was apprehensive about being in a school where almost everyone was unfamiliar. In all my previous years of schooling, either I knew the children present or my parents were acquainted with their families. And I always was aware that I was a Kaufman, and my family was respected in the community.

As I considered the vast differences in my schooling versus that of the students around me in the Berlin classroom, for a brief moment I wondered if I could readily meet their standards for completing the eighth grade. It was already so late in the year. Then I remembered that I had always easily accomplished the work I needed to do for school. I decided I could do so again.

At the end of the school day, my sisters came to meet me at my classroom door.

Fran's lips were tight as she declared, "The principal said the eighth-grade class was overcrowded, and since you already have a school to go to, you can't go to Berlin."

My face flushed as we silently hurried out of the building and to my sisters' car. I was disappointed but secretly also a little relieved. So much was changing so quickly, and I had little time to prepare myself for it. I wondered if I would fit in where almost everyone and everything were new. I didn't have to find out so soon.

I went back to Leeper for the last several months of the school year. I stayed to myself. I survived by knowing that I was getting out of "this backward place" in a few months and would soon be able to experience all sorts of exciting things in my new life.

New Clothes for Me

"Let's go buy some new clothes for you," Alma declared, smiling at me.

My mouth dropped open. "I'd love to," I told her.

Except for my underwear and stockings, I had never owned store-bought clothes before. I was fourteen years old, in the eighth grade, and visiting Alma for the weekend at her apartment on Larwill Street in Wooster, Ohio. I loved spending time with her. I always experienced something new.

But I also felt a bit uncomfortable with all the unfamiliarity in Alma's life. Sometimes she cooked foods I had never tasted before, like broccoli and cauliflower. I was not used to electric lights, music from a stereo, or wall-to-wall carpeting on floors. I was not used to sleeping in a house built just a few yards from other dwellings, with traffic going past at night, with train whistles blasting from across town. I was not used to the scent that permeated Alma's apartment—not a bad smell, but different from home. I was not used to accompanying my sister on visits to non-Amish friends who lived in non-Amish houses. And I had seldom spent the entire night away from our farm.

A few minutes after Alma suggested she and I go shopping, we stepped into her car and drove downtown. I smiled the whole way. In spite of all my efforts, I couldn't imagine wearing a dress made from a non-Amish pattern.

Alma parked her car near Freedlander's Department Store. She put coins in the meter, and we hurried inside. We took the elevator to the second floor, walked to the junior section, and began searching through the smaller sizes. A saleswoman offered to help us. Alma told her we wanted to buy clothes for me.

With a cool gaze, the saleswoman peered at me from head to toe, almost as if she were examining a piece of furniture. Then she declared, "I think we need to look in the preteen department," and marched toward a row of dresses twenty yards away.

Alma and I followed and began sorting through the clothes on the rack.

Suddenly I spotted a beautiful, filmy, pale blue dress. It had short, fitted sleeves and a full skirt with blue material that shimmered when light bounced across it. It was a dress beyond my dreams. With lips parted, I ran my fingers over the smooth fabric. Oblivious to my discovery, Alma continued examining one dress after another. Soon she pulled out a charcoal jumper paired with a white short-sleeved blouse. Red polka-dots were scattered across the blouse. It sported pearl buttons.

"I think this might fit you," Alma said as she held the outfit up for me to see.

The saleswoman carried the lovely blue dress, the charcoal jumper, and polka-dotted blouse into the fitting room. Alma and I followed her. My sister waited outside as I eagerly slipped into the shimmering blue dress. My cheeks flushed while I zipped up the back. Shivering, I twirled around and imagined myself at an elegant wedding. I stepped out of the dressing room and glided to a three-way mirror. Alma and the sales clerk inspected me.

"It is a pretty dress," Alma said. "Why don't you try on the jumper?"

I trudged to the dressing room and reluctantly tried on the polka-dotted blouse and the plain charcoal jumper. *I could easily make this jumper*, I thought. *The fabric is ordinary, and the style is ordinary.* The jumper was not in the same class as the blue dress. I walked back to the three-way mirror with Alma and the saleslady observing me.

"This fits you well," Alma noted. "But we'd have to get an additional blouse. Dad would have a fit if he saw you in this!" She looked at the polka-dotted blouse and grinned. "Do you have a plain-colored blouse that would go with this jumper?" she asked the saleswoman.

The salesclerk and Alma rummaged through a pile of blouses. Alma selected an orange-red one with short sleeves.

"This blouse is of much better quality than the polka-dotted one," Alma noted.

I returned to the dressing room, took off the polka-dotted blouse and the jumper, and put on the orange-red blouse. It was lovely, bright, a color I had never worn. My dark hair shone next to the fabric. I donned the jumper and walked out to the mirror. The outfit looked better than my Amish clothes, but it didn't shimmer.

"That's nice," Alma remarked. "I like it. And it's much more practical then the blue dress. Do you like it, Mary?"

I knew the jumper was more practical, because it was plainer. Still, I longed for the blue dress, which made me feel like dancing. I reminded myself that Alma was buying my new clothes, and I needed to be grateful for the outfit she wanted to give me. And I did admire the red blouse.

"I like it," I told Alma.

I went to the fitting room, took off the jumper and blouse, and put on my own clothes. I glanced at the exquisite blue dress, walked out the door, and handed the jumper and two blouses to Alma. She paid the clerk, who placed the clothes on two hangers and covered them with a long, plastic bag. We strolled to the elevator, rode downstairs, and walked out the door.

On Sunday evening, Alma drove me the fifteen miles home. When I walked into the house, I carried an opaque garment bag over my shoulder; I hurried into my bedroom and hung my clothes in the closet. I did not tell my parents about them.

HIGH SCHOOL AND COLLEGE

During high school and college, my major tasks were transitioning from childhood toward adulthood, adapting to an unfamiliar culture, and experimenting with how to be in this new world. It was a time of great excitement and also of pain and turmoil.

A Break in the Pattern

"Mom, may I wear non-Amish clothes to Celesta's wedding? I'm going to high school in three months, and I won't be wearing Amish clothes then. I don't want the kids I'll be going to high school with seeing me in Amish clothes."

My mother looked at me intently and then stood silently for a minute, staring into space. The wedding would take place in several weeks at the Mennonite church my cousin Celesta and her family attended. It was also the church I planned to join after starting high school. Many of the teenagers at the wedding would soon be my peers, and I did not want to stand out among them as odd and different.

Finally Mom said, "Let me talk with Dad."

I knew it was important to my mother that her children fit in socially. She came from a well-respected Amish family. Her Uncle Sol had been an esteemed bishop in the community. My mother had always fit in.

Later that afternoon, Mother emerged from her bedroom after consulting with my father for about ten minutes. She hesitated for a moment then slowly and, with determination, walked to the sofa where I was sitting. She looked me soberly in the eyes and said softly, "I guess you can wear what you want to the wedding."

"Thank you, Mom." I glowed. "I am so glad you let me!" I hurried to my bedroom and twirled around.

"I can wear non-Amish clothes," I whispered to myself, still twirling. "I can! I can! I can wear whatever I want. I am so happy…so happy!" I spun to the closet, grabbed one of my sister's dresses, held it against my body, and gazed into the mirror. I soon tossed the dress on the bed and seized another garment, grinning as I inspected my reflection again.

I was so happy my mother understood. I knew this decision came at a price for her and my father. My father's Amish siblings and their families would be at the wedding. The clothes I wore would provide evidence that the last of John and Susan's children was not adhering to the tradition. My mother's and father's parenting would be questioned, even if all maintained silence on the topic.

But my desire to wear non-Amish clothes was stronger than my concern for my parents' discomfort. I was simply happy that I could wear what I wished, that I would not stand out among my future fellow students.

I don't recall which dress I wore to the wedding. I only know it belonged to one of my sisters. I do remember how wonderful it felt to slide into the slippery back seat of my sister's car as we prepared to leave for the wedding. First my mother and then my father eased in beside me. I swiftly tugged to free my skirt from being wrinkled by my mother's dark dress.

I was dressed as I liked in the presence of my parents. I didn't have to hide.

But my mother hid her pain.

My Last Church Service

I slumped forward, trying to make myself comfortable on the hard wooden backless bench in John Fry's barn. I did not want to be there.

Earlier that morning when I protested going to church, my mother sternly insisted, "Mary, you have to go."

Scowling, I trudged to my room and stepped into my dark Amish dress. Because the garment had no buttons, I laboriously fastened it together at the side and in front with straight pins, pricking myself several times in the process. After finishing this ordeal, I grabbed my white organdy cape, draped it over my shoulders, crisscrossed the cloth on my chest (which signified I was single), and secured it in place with straight pins. Finally, I donned a dark one-stringed apron cut from the same fabric as my dress. I attached the apron to the dress with straight pins, as was the custom.

I felt foolish. I had never ever wanted to wear these grown-up clothes. They implied that I was now a young woman. The new apron, cape, and dress replaced both my child's frock, which buttoned in the back, and my full-length, white organdy apron, which was fastened at the nape of my neck with a little gold safety pin.

Now that I wore grown-up clothes, I was no longer allowed to leave my seat in the middle of church to fetch cookies and pretzels, nor could I sit on the bench with my mother. Instead, I was classified as one of the single women who filed into the church service according to age, the oldest leading. That meant I was one of the last girls in our row. At home I was the youngest and the child all my siblings doted on. I did not want to be at the bottom of the pecking order anywhere. Most unsettling of all, I had to sit with near-strangers, alone, for the entire three-hour service. For all of these reasons, I resisted grown-up clothes. But, under duress from my mother and sisters, I had been donning grown-up clothes for at least a season. I still disliked wearing them.

In the barn gentle breezes were floating through the giant, open doorway. I glanced outside and noticed my sisters' car speeding past on their way to the Mennonite church. I had already been sitting in church for a half hour. I yearned to be with Fran and Ada. Two and a half hours later, I glimpsed my sisters' car on their way home. I was still sitting in the same spot, daydreaming and gazing at the fields and trees in the distance. My backside smarted from the hardness of the bench, and my body ached to rush outside. My resolve became stronger; I vowed this would be the last time I ever attended the Amish church.

After the service, I wanted to get home as fast as I could. In a few weeks I would be attending high school and leaving the Amish way of life. Therefore, it seemed futile to further friendships with acquaintances from church. However, my parents always stayed for lunch, socializing for several hours. Today was no exception.

Several hours after church had ended, my mother, father, and I crawled into our buggy. I sighed with relief.

My father bid "Giddap" to Homer, our steady chestnut horse, and lightly tapped the reins. Homer ambled down the dirt lane toward our home.

As I hurried into our house, my sister Sarah sashayed across the living room toward me, smiling impishly. With a camera in her hand, she announced, "Mary, I want to take a picture of you."

I darted up the stairs and with a grim face declared, "You are not taking a picture of me in these clothes!" I dashed into my bedroom; seized the straight pins from my apron, cape, and dress; and tossed them onto my dresser. I slid out of my clothes and threw them on my bed. I was not ever going to wear them again. And I certainly didn't want a picture to memorialize that day.

Now I wish I could hold in my hand the photo that wasn't taken. I wonder what I looked like. I wonder what was whirling through my mind and heart other than my fervent desire to leave the Amish.

A New Person in Our House

When I was sixteen, Shirley came home from college with my sister Fran to live at our house for a year. Shirley had been my sister's roommate in college, and she and Fran were teaching elementary school in a nearby town.

Shirley was different. She was tall and slender and had short light brown hair that she curled at the ends.

Her full skirts were multicolored, and she wore lipstick. She spoke no Pennsylvania Dutch, nor did she understand it. She only spoke English and Platt Deutch.

Shirley sat at our table and ate our food. She smiled and joked. She teased my brothers and was kind and respectful to my mother. It didn't bother her that my parents were Amish or that my brothers, sisters, and I had been until just a few years before.

Shirley got along with everyone. Even my father liked her. That was important, because there would have been a lot of tension in our house if he didn't approve of her living with us. I think he enjoyed the newness that Shirley brought. My father appreciated the unusual.

I liked Shirley. She liked me too. She became my friend and was almost like another big sister. Sometimes when I was happy, I danced into Shirley's room. Often I brought several blouses and a skirt along with me. I would ask her which of the blouses looked best with the skirt I wanted to wear to school the next day.

She would look carefully at each one and say, "I like this one."

And then she would teach me about fashion by adding a question like, "Don't you think this color brings out the blue in the skirt?" Sometimes she also added a barrette to fix my hair. During our conversations, Shirley grinned at my budding interest in boys and helped me know how to be a teenager instead of a kid.

Shirley was not Amish, and she was not even a regular Mennonite. I had never known anyone like that before—at least not well. The feed salesman who came to our house every few months had never been Amish or Mennonite. And neither had the owners of the grocery store where our family shopped. But we only did business with them. We didn't socialize.

From Shirley I learned what people were like who had never been Amish. They laughed, they worked hard, they wore clothes they were used to, they teased, they were sad sometimes, they were kind and good. And I liked them.

Maybe I wasn't so different from people who weren't born Amish. Maybe we were more similar than different.

Becoming a Majorette

One summer day when I was sixteen, my sister Alma asked me, "Would you like to take baton lessons?"

I was stunned, then delighted. In my wildest dreams I never imagined taking baton lessons. I didn't know anyone who ever had.

"I would love to," I exclaimed.

Several weeks later, I arrived at Alma's apartment in Wooster, a town fifteen miles from home, for the first lesson. When I walked in the door, Alma smiled as she handed me a shiny silver baton with a white rubber cap on each end. It was beautiful.

I ran my hand the length of the smooth, glistening baton and looked at her with misty eyes. "Thank you," I whispered.

Alma said quickly, "It's time for you to leave for your lesson." She handed me money to pay for the instruction and a piece of paper with an address written on it.

She gave me directions. "Walk to Market Street. Then turn right and go until you get to this address," she instructed. "It's about five blocks from here, the second-to-last house before you get to the high school."

I changed into a pair of my sister's jeans because I had none of my own, hurried out of the house, turned left, and walked swiftly up the street. The sun was shining brightly, and my body was tense.

I arrived at the address on the piece of paper. In front of me stood a house unlike any dwelling in my home community. It was painted dark brown and had an arched front door. The bottom edges of the roof curved in toward the outside walls of the house like a freshly coifed pageboy. I cautiously walked up the driveway and rang the doorbell. A beautiful young woman opened the door. She was several years older than I, with dark hair, brown sparkling eyes, bright red lipstick, and lovely tanned legs appearing beneath white shorts. She said hello and welcomed me. Then she led me to the blacktop behind her house, and our lesson began.

My teacher chatted easily and then became serious. I stood facing her as she demonstrated the day's lesson in slow motion.

"Grasp the baton in the middle with your right hand—the large rubber tip should be on the left—and move your hand so the tip makes a figure eight in front of your body," she said.

My hand felt slow and awkward as I attempted to follow her directions and make the unfamiliar movements. I dropped the baton repeatedly.

"When you learn to do it very fast, it will look like this." She grinned as she spun her baton so rapidly that all I could see was a shiny circular glimmer. Then she showed me how to make the figure eight in front of my body with my left hand, on each side of my body, and above my head.

At the end of the session, she wrote directions for the figure eight in large, rounded, clear print on a half sheet of stiff almond-colored paper. "Practice this week," she said.

My legs moved effortlessly in long strides as I returned to Alma's house, smiling all the way. I swung my baton as I went. The world was mine to experience. *I* had a baton lesson. *I* was going to learn how to twirl a baton.

I took lessons each week for the rest of the summer. At home in the front yard, I practiced twirling my baton. My mother observed from the kitchen window and my father from the porch. He admired my ability to throw the baton high in the air and to continue twirling without dropping it. My mom said nothing but didn't seem upset. However, I practiced marching steps in my bedroom, because I knew my parents wouldn't approve of those. Twirling was a skill, but in my parents' eyes, marching would only draw unwelcome attention to my body.

Early one morning before classes started, I went to speak with Mr. Miller, the band director, while he was preparing for music class. For the previous twenty-four hours, I had practiced what I wanted to say to him.

"I have been taking baton lessons this summer and would like to be a majorette," I sputtered.

Mr. Miller, who knew my father, did not indicate in any way that my request might be strange. He simply asked from whom I had taken baton lessons. I told him. At his bidding, I showed him my skills in twirling. After observing me, he told me to show up for band practice later in the week.

I was in, and I was elated. I, who had been Amish a little more than a year ago, was going to be a majorette. I could hardly believe it was true.

Several weeks later, all the majorettes were measured for costumes in one of our homes. Another majorette's mother and a friend of hers encircled each of us with tape measures at strategic places and wrote down figures. I tried to imagine my mother being present and couldn't. My face felt warm and flushed. I had never before been measured for any clothing like this.

I returned to the majorette's home to try on my costume. It looked foreign to me and not as polished as I had expected. The gold braid sewn on the bodice of the white satin outfit seemed too thin. The costume didn't appear well pressed, and it looked homemade to me. However, the underside of my short, flared skirt was a rich gold. I reminded myself that the costume wasn't finished and probably would look better when it was completed. A few days later Alma took me to a store near her house to buy white majorette boots. The school gave me a white hat with a gold plume, as well as a white tassel to attach to the front of each boot near the top.

After arriving home with my new outfit, I slipped into it and stood on my bed so I could see myself in the mirror. Someone else seemed to be grinning back at me. The only familiar part of the person in the mirror was her face. I looked good. I was euphoric that this beautiful costume was mine but scared that this time I might be going too far. I was wearing an outfit like no Kaufman had ever worn.

I did not tell my parents anything about my new pursuit. I am sure they knew at least a part of what I was doing, but they said nothing.

My sister Sarah gave me a permanent a few days before my first performance. When we took the rollers out of my shoulder-length dark hair, it was as straight as it had been before we started. I was disheartened, because I wanted everything to be just right. Sarah continued to work with my hair, finally plaiting it into two braids and wrapping each braid like a jelly roll around the side of my head. I carefully put my hat on, grabbed a hand mirror, and checked myself out as I slowly turned around in front of our dresser mirror. I looked almost Asian with my unusual hairstyle, well-tanned body, and high cheek bones. I was glad the perm didn't take.

I was dressed and ready for the performance, and I did not look Amish.

I put on my long coat in my bedroom and left the house immediately. I did not want my parents to see what I was wearing, because I knew they would not like it.

My school did not have a football team, so the band played at halftime during basketball games. The gym was so small that it was once described in a newspaper article as being the size of a cracker box. But it seemed plenty big to me. I felt excited, anxious, and shy as I entered the school in my costume and new hairstyle. I hoped I would twirl well and keep my baton from dropping.

At halftime the other majorettes and I gathered at the entrance to the gym with the band members behind us. We stood at attention with our left hands on our waists and our right hands holding the balls of our batons. Mr. Miller raised his arms, and with a quick downward movement of his hands, the familiar music started. Beginning with our right legs up and our toes down, we marched into the gym, swinging our batons.

I felt exhilarated as I looked around and saw familiar faces in the audience. *I* was a majorette, and I liked it. I knew the movements well. But several times as I reached to grab my baton from where I had hurled it high into the air, I missed it. Each time I snatched it from the floor and continued. I hated dropping my baton, but it didn't seem like a terrible blunder, because the other majorettes occasionally dropped theirs also. When the show was over and we marched out of the gym, I was relieved that it had gone reasonably well. My mind raced, and my body trembled. I wished the performance had not finished so soon.

When I arrived home, I felt conflicted. I wanted to continue being a majorette, because it gave me a unique role in my school. It helped me belong somewhere in the new world I had chosen. Classmates spoke to me who previously had not.

I was never sure how much my parents knew about my majorette activities. I cannot remember my mother ever talking with me about it, but I did know that what she was cognizant of pained her. It troubled me.

At least my father partially supported me. I heard him telling a salesman, "My daughter can throw a baton high in the air and catch it. I don't know how she does it."

I also knew the neighbors and relatives looked upon my parents negatively because of what I was doing and thought I should be controlled better. I didn't care much what the neighbors and relatives thought about me. But I did care if they slighted my parents because of my actions. In the end, my enjoyment of twirling was stronger than these worries about my parents, and I continued being a majorette.

Years later Alma revealed that the reason she offered me baton lessons was to try to help me avoid the community's prejudice toward our Amish background. She didn't want me to be held back by discrimination.

The Bishop Speaks

It was a day like any other. I went to school, attended classes, did my lessons, talked with my friends on the way home, and looked forward to seeing my sister when I got off the bus at the end of the route.

My sister Sarah drove me to the bus stop every morning and picked me up every afternoon, because no one else from our Amish neighborhood went to high school, and the bus's nearest stop was three miles from our house.

When I met her that afternoon, her face was grim. "JJ came to see Mom and Dad today," she said.

I looked at her with surprise. JJ was the bishop of the Mennonite church my sisters, brothers, and I attended. (My parents were still Amish.) As far as I knew, JJ had never been to our house before.

She continued angrily, "He said you can't be baptized unless you quit being a majorette."

My chest became tight and my face hot. I was speechless.

Finally I gasped. "He says I can't be a majorette?"

I had sensed that some people from the church disapproved of my costume's short skirt and the bare legs it revealed, but none of them had ever said a word to me about it. The tradition in the church was for women to dress modestly, to have sleeves in their dresses, to wear their hair long, and to cover their heads when praying. (Men made the rules. There were no expectations for them to dress differently than non-Mennonites.) As a result, no one my age or older had ever been a cheerleader or a majorette. However, the youth in the church were pushing the boundaries. Two girls a few years younger than me were cheerleaders and seemed appreciated for it. They were from well-established families in the church.

"He said majorettes wear too-skimpy clothes, and there will be no majorettes in the church," Sarah said indignantly. She quickly continued, "I was in the kitchen listening and wanted to tell him there are lots of boys in the church who are on the basketball team and a couple of girls who are cheerleaders, and their clothes are just as skimpy as majorettes' outfits."

She paused and then continued with anger in her voice. "He said someone from the church talked with him about seeing your picture in the paper last week and was upset about it."

JJ had earlier told one of my siblings, that because we came from the Amish, he expected us to be examples to others in the church.

I was hurt and furious. I believed JJ was being very unfair.

When I arrived home, the lines were tight on my parents' faces. Neither said anything to me about the visit from JJ. Because of that, I knew two things: first, my parents felt what he was requiring of me was unfair, and second, they would not try to influence my decision about whether or not to be baptized.

For three days I struggled. I knew the church was being discriminatory, and therefore, I believed, ungodly. Having separate expectations and rules for someone who came from the Amish was wrong. When I left the Amish, joining the Mennonite church was the only acceptable alternative for me or for my parents. Now, if I did not become baptized, I would not be a full member of the congregation. I wanted a sense of belonging to a spiritual group.

People who did not belong to a church were treated politely in my community but were only associated with in business dealings unless they were family. Also, my classmates had been baptized several years before when I was still Amish. I already felt different from them, not to mention disoriented as a result of all the changes I had made in the last several years. I would feel even more alone if I started to attend another church by myself. I needed to belong to the world I had chosen to enter. I finally decided to quit being a majorette.

The next Sunday I slipped into a beautiful white dress embossed with pale silvery flowers. Sarah had made it for me to wear to my baptism. I felt sick. Sarah and I drove to the church in silence. As advised, I sat in a pew near the front of the church.

When it was time for the baptism, JJ made a short speech, ending with, "There will be no majorettes in the church."

Then he called me and another person up to be baptized. I was mortified. I walked to the front of the church, knelt as directed in front of JJ, and he sprinkled water on my head declaring, "In the name of the Father, and the Son, and the Holy Spirit…"

No one from the church ever again talked with me about what had happened, nor did I initiate a conversation regarding it. I became an official member that Sunday, but I never felt as if I belonged during all the eight years I attended. I continued to be an outsider.

It is fifty-some years since then. The story of my baptism still tastes like sour milk to me, and I feel sad at the intensity of not belonging that I experienced during my teen years. I remind myself that I also have good memories of some people in that church. In particular,

I fondly remember several close girlfriends, and especially their mothers, who were unusually kind to me.

But still, whenever I drive past the church where I attended, a dull ache oozes from the pit of my stomach. My foot automatically presses harder on the accelerator of my car. The appearance of the church belies my feelings. It looks peaceful in the midst of the countryside, as it did when I began attending there at age fourteen. The church is still painted white. The property looks a little more prosperous. A large addition has been constructed, and there is a fellowship hall at the end of the parking area. Elegant houses have been built nearby.

I am also aware the reasons I chose to be baptized were probably more because "that is what one does" than for strong spiritual reasons.

Speech Lessons Required

"The education department has decided that you need to take speech lessons," declared Dr. Umble, the head of the speech department at my college.

I was astonished. Why would the education department want me to take speech lessons? I knew I didn't need to speak more clearly in order to teach. People understood me perfectly well when I talked. In fact, I excelled in speech. I had placed third in a countywide speech contest in high school and in a poetry reading contest in college. I also had won leading female roles in one high school and two college plays. I had received many compliments for my performances. Because of my success in speech and drama, I was puzzled at Dr. Umble's suggestion that I take speech lessons. But maybe lessons would help my words flow more smoothly. Plus, I loved all things connected with speech.

Dr. Umble looked at me somberly and directly. He continued, "I don't agree with the education department and tried to convince them that you do not need speech lessons. I told them a Pennsylvania Dutch accent is not any different than a southern accent or a New York accent." He paused. "They disagree. You and your brother are the only ones in the department required to take speech lessons. They said you cannot do your student teaching until you complete them."

I was dumbfounded that the education department thought my way of speaking was not good enough. But I knew that if I spoke with no trace of an accent, I would feel more as if I belonged. And it might be fun to take speech lessons. It was something I had never done before.

"I'll take speech lessons," I told Dr. Umble.

Dr. Umble flattened his lips, extending the corners of his mouth in an unconscious gesture common for him when he was dealing with a precise matter. He was a short, small-framed, handsome, and intense gray-haired man. Dr. Umble directed the plays I was in and had chosen me for a part each time I auditioned. He was forthright in expecting students to do their best, but I never saw him treat anyone unkindly. He was my favorite professor.

He and I arranged a time to meet for my first lesson.

"Put the tip of your tongue between your teeth when you say the 'th' sound," Dr. Umble told me. He demonstrated, softly saying "them" and "the".

At first I had difficulty hearing the difference in sound when my tongue was hitting my teeth instead of in the front of the roof of my mouth. But then I heard it.

I practiced each week between lessons. It felt awkward to twist my tongue into new positions to say words I had said thousands of times before. But I was grateful for help in becoming free from prejudice. I wanted to speak like everyone else. I did not want to stand out because I used to be Amish.

Only recently, as I began exploring the events of my young adulthood, did I become acutely aware that the requirement for me to take speech lessons was a form of prejudice. At the time the discrimination occurred, it would have been too painful and damaging for me to fully acknowledge it. However, I did feel embarrassed about having to take speech lessons and kept it to myself. Although I loved learning more about speech, I hated being seen as not "good enough" because of my culture. I was proud of my heritage.

My mother, Susan Schlabach, when she was in about the fifth grade. (Photographer unknown.)

One summer in his youth my father, John M. Kaufman, and several of his friends followed the harvest west, working as they found jobs. He had this picture taken on his trip. (Photographer unknown.)

I have very few pictures of myself as a child. This is my favorite. Because my siblings and I were going raspberry picking, I was allowed to wear a pair of my brother Sam's old pants and shirt to protect myself from the sharp thorns. It was usually the only time I was allowed to wear long pants.

Front row: Me and Sam. Back row: Ada
and Fran. Raspberry picking day.

Leo used to tease my mother. Here
they are tussling in the kitchen.

After taking some classes at Eastern Mennonite High School, Alma took the GED and entered Eastern Mennonite College. (Photographer unknown.)

Alma had more conflict with my parents than the rest of us because she was the first in the family to leave the Amish. I found this photo lying face down in a drawer in Alma's house after she died.

Mother and Dad often sat on the front porch on summer evenings. I think they were surprised that this picture was being taken.

This is my favorite picture of my mother.
She looks the most as I remember her.

When my siblings and I came home on vacation we often played games. Here we are playing Chinese checkers. Clockwise: my brother-in-law Bob Gerber, Fran, (who is married to Bob), me, Sam, Mother, and Dad.

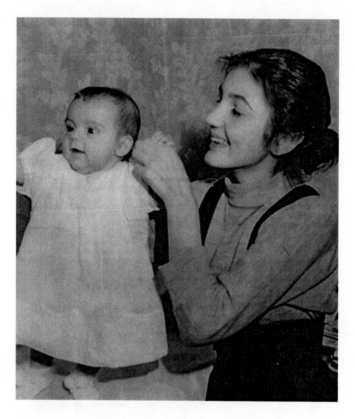

My siblings and I were very excited when my brother Leo and his wife, Ada, had children. They were our first nieces and nephews. Here I am holding my niece Debbie.

Front row: Fran holding Debbie, Mother holding Gary, Dad holding Steve, and Ada (Leo's wife) holding Vicky. Back row: Allen, Ada, Leo, Sarah, and Alma.

Dad.

My brother Leo didn't like us to mess with his car. However, he would occasionally ask my sisters or me to clean the inside. I always liked to be present when his car was being cleaned, because then we could turn on the radio and listen to country music.

(Photo used with permission by Robert Hinshaw.) My son, Christopher, and I when he was about two and a half years old, shortly before we returned to the States after living in Switzerland for over three and a half years.

Alma. (Photographer unknown.)

Siblings and in-laws. Front row: Ada K. (Leo's widow), me, Sarah, Alma, Mary Ellen (Allen's widow). Second row: Larry (my husband), Ada, Joan (Sam's wife), Sam, Fran, and Bob (Fran's husband).

In 1999 all my siblings and I went to Brazil for our nephew Joe's wedding. Sarah, Fran, me, and Ada.

Partial family photo in 2010. Front row: Audrey, Sophia, and Madeleine. Second row: Christopher, me, Larry, Will, Jeremy, and Abby. (Photo used with permission by Stephen Reason.)

Larry and me. (Photo used with permission by Tom Forrest.)

YOUNG ADULTHOOD

Excitement and delight coexisted with pain in my young adult years as I worked to establish myself. It was a time of developing independence, dealing with my mother's death, getting married, living in a foreign country, giving birth to my son, getting a divorce, earning my Ph.D., and settling into a career.

Mother's Illness and Death

When I was twenty-two, my mother became sick. She died five months after the first signs of her illness appeared. Mother had lung cancer. She had feared getting cancer ever since she watched her father's very painful death from the disease when she was twenty-six.

My mother coughed a lot when my brothers, sisters, and I were at home in Ohio for Christmas in 1964. Several days after Christmas in the middle of the afternoon, I walked into the kitchen to get a drink of water and discovered her. She was standing with her back to the stove coughing blood into a white handkerchief.

I was alarmed and questioned her, "How long have you been coughing blood? Have you seen Dr. Patterson?"

She quietly said the blood had been appearing for a few weeks, and no, she had not discussed it with Dr. Patterson. She gazed at the wall in front of her as she minimized her symptoms, murmuring, "It's probably nothing."

I told her, "You need to make an appointment with Dr. Patterson to make sure," and walked back into the living room to continue talking with my sisters. I don't remember whether or not I told them Mother had been coughing up blood. I didn't want to believe Mother was ill.

After the holidays I returned to Indiana, where I taught fifth grade. About a month later, my roommate and I visited my sister Fran and her husband, Bob, who lived an hour away in Nappannee where he was a minister at a Mennonite church. As soon as we stepped out of the car, Fran greeted us in the driveway. She began talking about Dad's postcard, which stated Mother had lung cancer and only a few months to live.

I was bewildered and muttered, "What are you talking about?"

Fran peered at me and asked, "Didn't you get a postcard from Dad?" I told her I hadn't.

I later discovered that my father had sent a card to each of his children, but somehow mine arrived a week late.

As I listened to my sister tell me about Mother's imminent death, my body went numb, and my thoughts whirled. It was inconceivable to think of my mother dying, of her simply not being there. To not have a mother would be horrifying. No one close to me had ever died before. I had only been to three funerals in my life.

Over the next few months, my siblings and I spent as much time with Mother as we possibly could. My oldest sister, Alma, took a leave of absence from her job and moved home to take care of Mother. Fran and I lived and worked in Indiana and were only able to visit our mother on weekends. On countless Friday evenings, my roommate, Joan, drove me to meet Fran at a designated spot between her house and mine. Fran and I then traveled the 250 miles home to Ohio in Fran's Beetle Volkswagen.

When Fran and I went home at first, Mother continued cooking meals, sewing, and cleaning the house. But within a few weeks, such activity often forced her to gasp for breath. So she often sat in her overstuffed chair for two or three hours at a time. Six or seven weeks later, she was bedridden.

Mother was not ready to die. After having been pregnant for ninety months of her life, bearing ten children—two of whom died at birth—rearing eight children, canning, cooking, sewing, cleaning, and seldom venturing from the house for months at a time (except for church), my mother was finally free of heavy household obligations. She had time to read magazines, to visit with friends and relatives, to go shopping with Dad rather than just giving him a list. Throughout the years, whenever Mother talked about traveling, I had detected a yearning in her voice. My father did not like to sleep in any bed but his own, so she had not left the state until shortly before I went to college. Once or twice a year, my parents traveled to Indiana with me or one of my siblings to visit Fran.

I had hardly ever seen my mother angry, but she fought her coming death. She was angry that no one could think of a way to beat the cancer. She was incredulous that the doctors didn't at least try some treatment. She was convinced that she was being left to die. And my mother, who had rarely raised her voice in my presence, began to voice her feelings of frustration, sadness, and anger to Alma.

My mother changed in other ways as well. Before developing cancer she had almost always sacrificed her desires for those of others. Now there were moments when she gave priority to her own wishes. A religious relative came to "evangelize" her, asking if she was "saved."

Mother told Alma, "If she comes again, I don't want to see her."

After that, my sister guarded Mother's privacy carefully. When the woman visited again, Alma invited her into the house but didn't let her see my mother.

In addition, Mother no longer seemed to care whether or not her head was covered. Before Mother's cancer, I had never seen her head uncovered except when she was combing her hair. Her daytime clothing had always included a white organdy cap. Before going to bed, she put on a long, white organdy scarf, which had become soft from many washings. But now there were days when she didn't cover her head. To my amazement, being bareheaded didn't seem to bother Mother.

More than ever before, my mother did what she felt was right for her. She no longer appeared to care what the neighbors thought.

During one of my last visits home, I sat on a chair next to Mother's bed in the mid-afternoon.

Suddenly Mother looked intently at me and said, "Mary, it doesn't matter if the person you choose to marry is considered important by others. He doesn't have to do big things." She paused a moment and continued, "It only matters that he is good to you—that he is kind and an honorable person."

I was taken aback by her statement, and I don't remember responding to it. My mother didn't usually initiate conversation about such intimate subjects, so I knew she was trying to forewarn me against possible misfortune. And now, after many more years of living, I also know she was simply trying to take care of me before she died.

The last time I saw my mother, she was very ill. Throughout my visit, she hardly ate, and her energy was gone. Before returning to Indiana, I went to her bed. She painstakingly sat up in her rumpled white nightgown, gazing at me. We hugged. Tears ran down our faces.

I told her, "I will be back next weekend."

My mother said, "It won't matter."

I was stunned and told her, "It matters to me."

She died that week.

I don't remember how I traveled home for my mother's funeral. When I arrived at my parents' house, my sisters told me that several neighbor women had gone to the funeral home. My mother's body had been taken there from the hospital. She had died in the middle of the night with my brother Sam holding her hand. They told me that at the funeral home, the neighbor women would be fixing Mother's hair and dressing her body in clothes my sisters had selected from her closet. My family and I waited at home.

Later that day, a black hearse rolled into our driveway. One of my siblings held the front door of the house open as I stood with my brothers and sisters, our father, and several neighbors, tearfully watching through the doorway. As if drawn by a magnet, my eyes centered on the coffin in the back of the hearse. One of the attendants walked toward the house carrying a coffin stand. My sister directed him to my parents' bedroom; their bed had been dismantled and moved to the basement. After the attendant returned to the hearse, he and his partner pulled the closed pine coffin, handmade by an Amish carpenter, out of the back of the vehicle. They slowly carried it through our yard, up the steps, onto the porch, in the front door, through the living room, and into my parents' bedroom.

Then they carefully opened the top third of the coffin. A few at a time, my father, brothers, and sisters entered the bedroom, stayed a few minutes, and came back visibly shaken. I waited until last. After taking a deep breath, I also entered the bedroom. Tears rolled down my cheeks as I peered at my mother's face. Without her smile, her face seemed stiff and only vaguely familiar. I could tolerate only a few minutes with her body and soon turned and walked out of the room.

Relatives, neighbors, and friends filled our house, porch, and yard. Everyone wore black. Neighbors set up several backless wooden benches in the living room to make space for people to sit. Throughout the day, women from the community knocked on our door, bringing pies, cakes, and casseroles they had prepared. When mealtime approached, the same women served this food to everyone present. People came to our house that I had not seen for years. Others came that I had often heard about but never met, including Ida, a beloved former housekeeper.

As the evening wore on, everyone went home except two neighbor women. As was customary in the Amish culture, they stayed to sit with my mother's body throughout the night. I put on my pajamas and crawled into bed but spent much of the next eight hours tossing and turning. Only a wall separated me from my mother's dead body in the adjoining room.

My mother was buried a day before her sixty-fifth birthday. I can recall only a few details about the funeral. I remember that it was a beautiful, warm day. I remember the simple black dress I had made and wore. I remember filing into the church with my family, following Mother's coffin. I remember tossing a ball in our yard late that afternoon. I remember wanting to go into the house to tell my mother something and then realizing with a jolt that she was not there.

I grieved for my mother. I was angry and sad about her death. I missed her terribly. She would never again be there to greet me when I came home. Her house would be unkempt and empty. There would be no more letters from her. I knew that my unborn children would never know their grandmother. Her place was vacant.

Five months after my mother died, all of my brothers, sisters, nieces, and nephews met at my parents' house for Thanksgiving with my father. As we gathered at the table for dinner, I was acutely aware of the empty seat next to Dad. We started to sit down, and Alma, who arrived at the table last, gingerly sat in my mother's chair. We bowed our heads to pray. A long yearning silence engulfed our whole family as we felt the emptiness created by Mother's absence.

For Christmas that year, I wrapped my gifts in black paper with thin, colored lines. I did not plan it so. It was simply the only paper that felt appropriate.

A year after my mother died, I moved to Washington, DC. While there, I visited and revisited Picasso's blue paintings at the National Gallery of Art. As I gazed at the paintings, I knew that I was not alone in my pain. Strangely, I felt comforted. Several years later when I traveled to Italy, I lit a candle for my mother in a cathedral in Florence.

The ache has eased during the forty-six years since my mother died. Now when I think of her, I remember her fondly with little distress. But occasionally tears still come to my eyes. Perhaps it will always be that way.

Independence in the City

I left Dupont Circle on my way home from work and sauntered up the shady sidewalk of New Hampshire Avenue toward 16th Street. The weather was hot and sultry. My light blue, straight mini-skirted dress clung to me. I could have taken the bus home, but it would have cost more money than I wanted to spend. My budget was tight, and walking didn't hurt me. At 16th Street I headed north.

Within a few blocks, I arrived at 2120 16th Street Northwest, my home. I strode up the semi-circular driveway, smiled as I opened one of the glass front doors, and stepped into the comfortable air-conditioned lobby of my apartment building.

Behind the front desk, the well-dressed, gray-haired clerk beamed as she greeted me with her Southern drawl, saying, "No mail today."

After chatting with her briefly, I pushed the elevator's up button. When the door slid open a moment later, I hurried inside. Within seconds I was unlocking the door to my apartment.

I stepped onto the dark wooden parquet floor and flipped on the light. I closed my eyes and breathed in the air. This was my space. Mine alone.

I strolled into the dressing room, threw off my clothes, and turned on the tap in my square bathtub. As the water gushed out, I ambled into the kitchen, poured myself a glass of chilled orange juice, carried it into the bathroom, and set it on the edge of my tub. I loved my square bathtub and large dressing room. They made my efficiency apartment seem spacious.

After lounging in the tub for a quarter hour, my stomach began to growl. Within minutes I was in my tiny kitchen preparing my evening meal. I carried my dinner to the sofa, turned on the television, and sat down just in time for my nightly date with Walter Cronkite.

I loved my freedom. For the first time in my life, I could do just what I wanted without having to be accountable to anyone but myself. Except for one thing. Before I moved to the city I promised my father I would not walk on the streets after dark by myself. I had no family in town, no roommate, and only friends of my own choosing. I could comb the racks at Woodward and Lothrup for beautiful clothes. I could stroll along the sidewalks of Georgetown gazing at gorgeous colors and bizarre shapes in shop windows. I could invite friends over to lounge on bright cushions while dining at my foot high, thirty-six inch square table, and we could drink tea until late into the night. I could stroll through the National Museum of Art on a Saturday for the whole day if I chose. I could meander down the Ellipse with a friend and have a picnic on the mound leading to the Washington Memorial. I could attend classes at the Church of the Saviour and, without raising an eyebrow, question the basic religious beliefs I had been indoctrinated in since birth. I could volunteer to serve coffee and sandwiches at the Potter's House on Saturday nights with a group of my friends. I could be in a therapy group. I could think my own thoughts without anyone from my tradition influencing me. No one knew my family. I was my own person.

When I walked down the streets of Washington, DC, I heard people of many nationalities speak languages I had never heard before. The unusual was normal. I did not feel different. It was my city, and I was at home.

Leaving the Country

Everything around me appeared surreal—the ship's white metal siding, smooth and cool beneath my palm; the people bustling to find their cabins; the murky waters of New York Harbor. How could it be that I was here? I was a little Amish girl who grew up on a farm in the Midwest. My mother didn't travel out of the state of Ohio until I was almost ready for college. When I was a child, no one would have guessed that I would travel to foreign lands, and few would have supposed that I wanted such an opportunity. I felt exceedingly fortunate.

My husband and I were on a ship named *The United States*, ready to depart for Europe. He was going to study, and I planned to find a job. We had been preparing for months, saving every penny possible, emptying our retirement accounts, applying for visas, packing our books and suitcases, finding storage places for belongings left behind, transferring the title of our dark green Triumph. One of my most important tasks was deciding which reminders of home to take. I chose a petite pottery vase, a blue pottery bowl, and family photos. In my pocket I also carried a small, rough rock, which I carefully selected from my father's driveway the last time I visited home.

Finally, August 28, 1969, had come. That morning four friends with two cars heaped our luggage into their trunks and drove us from New Haven, Connecticut, to New York City. We were all on board the ship. Our friends laughed and joked. One of them poured champagne into paper cups and passed the drinks around. We lifted our cups, and they saluted our journey.

My husband and I would travel by ship for five days until we reached Le Havre in France. We would then board three trains in two days: the first would take us to Paris, the second was an overnight train to Basel, and the third would deliver us to Zurich, where we would live. Years in Switzerland would give us many wonderful opportunities. We would make new friends. We would climb mountains, have picnics in the parks, and perhaps learn to ski. In a month or two we would travel to Wurzburg, Germany, where my husband had relatives. And if we could find a way to finance a trip to Portugal, we would visit friends there. I wanted to taste the foods in France, explore the Black Forest in Germany, and hear Italian spoken in Italy.

My thoughts whirled. How could I live so far from my family for two full years? If I couldn't afford to fly home for a visit in two years, perhaps I would even be gone for four. I couldn't imagine being away for so long; I had always spent Christmas at home. My husband was the only family member I'd have, and we'd only met two years before. I was overwhelmed by the totality of the unfamiliar facing me but delighted with all the new adventures I would have.

Our friends gave us hugs and waved as they walked off the ship and down the sidewalk. With a loud clang, the gangplank was pulled up. We leaned against the railing while our ship slowly and quietly glided out of New York Harbor. We watched as the Statue of Liberty and the skyscrapers became smaller and smaller. The quiet calm of the ocean engulfed us.

We were off to a new land, to unknown customs, to an unfamiliar language, to a new life!

Similar Language, New Respect

I quickly stepped onto the tram at Banhofstrasse, dropped my token into the fare box, spied an empty seat, and sat down. I smiled to myself, pleased that I was finding my way around Zurich alone after arriving only a few weeks ago. Most seats were full. Passengers appeared exceptionally proper, as evidenced by their stalwart bearing, neat coiffures, and attractive, well-coordinated clothes. I marveled at how clean the tram was. Not a speck of paper or dust was evident. The people around me were staring straight ahead, seemingly in their own worlds.

Suddenly, catty-corner from me, an impeccably dressed middle-aged gentleman began speaking in German to a man facing him. My cheeks instantly flushed. I started breathing rapidly. Didn't they know that talking German in public invited ridicule? I glanced up the aisle at the other passengers. No one appeared to notice the two men, who were the only people talking out loud. Both men looked powerful and prosperous, their fashionable dark suits, broad silk ties, starched white shirts, and shiny wing-tip shoes were a cut above every other traveler's attire.

It didn't make sense to me. Where I came from, speaking a German dialect fluently in public was something to hide if you wanted to be a part of the non-Amish teenage and young adult world.

Idealization or Discrimination

Our friend stopped his fork in midstream, his blue eyes round and piercing, "You used to be Amish?"

I reiterated that I was born into an Amish family.

He continued staring at me, and then remarked, "May I touch you?"

In the deafening silence, my stomach contracted and my face reddened. *I don't belong in a zoo.*

Our friend had known my husband and me for months, if not years. We occasionally had dinner with him and his wife. That night we were sitting around their dining room table in a small town outside Zurich.

In the community where I grew up, I was discriminated against because I was born Amish. In the outside world, I tended to be idealized because I once was Amish. I wanted neither. I only wanted to be treated as a normal human being.

A New Beginning

My husband went home to call his parents.

A white-clad nurse assisted me as I struggled from the delivery bed into the regular hospital bed. With a gentle smile, she handed my newly born son to me. He was swaddled in a soft white flannel blanket. Only his head stuck out. Abundant, unruly straight black hair burst from his scalp. His face was red, and his whole body was scrunched up, almost as if he were still enclosed in my womb. I was amazed at how beautiful he was. I had always heard that babies were ugly when they were born, but my baby was beautiful! He snuggled in my arms—or perhaps I snuggled with him. My baby felt surprisingly unfamiliar, considering that he had already been with me for nine months.

In her thick Swiss German accent, the nurse declared, "We are taking you to your room."

The wide door swung open, and she began rolling us out of the delivery room and into the silent white corridor of the hospital. There were only three of us: the nurse, my son, and myself. I felt as if we were in the most wonderful parade imaginable. It was of no concern to me that we had no audience. All that mattered was that I was with my son. Traveling into the hallway made his birth public.

The nurse rolled us into a small private room painted white. After positioning the bed, she left the room, saying, "I will come in a few minutes to get your baby."

I continued lying in bed, holding my son, staring at his face in amazement. I glided my finger across his soft cheek and into a tuft of his fine hair, which stood on end. Occasionally he made a faint baby sound.

I whispered his name, "Christopher." It seemed strange to call my baby by his name. I gazed at him some more. He was perfect.

The nurse soon arrived, and I reluctantly handed my son to her.

She stated, "I am taking him to the nursery. You will see him in the morning. Get some sleep—you have had a hard day."

I watched her walk out the door holding him in her arms.

Propped up in bed, I lay for hours taking in what had just happened. I knew it was momentous. My life would be forever changed. We had a son. I was a mother. My husband was a father. We were a family.

I imagined what my son's life might be like as he slowly grew from one year to the next. I realized that he would become part of contemporary Western culture, that he would have no experience of living in the Amish world into which I had been born. I suddenly knew that now I too belonged to the culture that would be his. For the first time since I left the Amish, I no longer felt as if I was straddling the fence between two worlds.

Another cog inside of me settled into place.

My Tsunami

The tsunami in my life was my divorce. No one in my immediate or extended family had ever chosen to end their marriage. I had never known anyone who was in the process of going through a divorce. My closest family member lived hundreds of miles away. In addition, my husband, son, and I had moved to Houston only about a year before our separation. I knew few people and did not have close relationships, which take long periods of time to develop. Furthermore, I was a stay -at-home mom and did not have an automatic outlet for meeting people or providing for myself financially.

However, over the years I learned a great deal from the experience of my divorce.

1. No matter how much one person tries to nurture a relationship, it will wither and die unless both partners prioritize and attend to it.

2. Continually giving without attending to one's own needs results in losing oneself.

3. I am defined by who I am and not by someone's perception of me.

4. No matter how painful and destructive a divorce is, it is important to let go of the anger and move on.

5. It is possible to be happy again.

6. A first marriage that ends in divorce can be followed by a happy second marriage.

Evading My Reflection

I walked with Alma into her church and was surprised to see John again. He was dressed in a handsome black suit and a red tie. His hair was attractively cut in a contemporary style. John wore glasses. He talked easily. He had completed college, and I think had earned his doctorate. Married and a father, John taught the Sunday school class Alma and I attended.

With pain in his voice, John disclosed to the class the intense alienation he had experienced from his fellow high school students. It was clear the distress lingered with him.

I knew John's pain. It was like my own.

I remembered him from forty years earlier.

I saw John walking down the steps as I was going up. His face was drawn and tense. A few faint freckles scattered across his baby cheeks. He looked down and then straight ahead. He was neatly dressed in blue barn-door pants, matching suspenders, and a light-colored short-sleeved shirt. His dark hair was cut Amish style. He was a handsome boy, about my height, and a freshman in high school.

I had never seen John talk to any of his fellow students, or walk down the hall with friends. He was always alone. I knew John was interesting and smart. Any Amish student with the gumption to attend high school had to possess an intense desire to explore the world beyond the community. John had to want to be in high school so badly that he was willing to attend, even though his parents required him to wear Amish clothes. He and his brother were the only students at the high school donning Amish garb. His brother was one year ahead of me and at the top of his class.

I felt uncomfortable whenever I saw John. Misery engulfed his face. Still, I never talked with him nor said hello. Instead, I made sure I was never seen near him. Since John was a freshman and I was a senior, it was easy for me to avoid him. I already felt discriminated against because I grew up Amish. If I hung around anyone else who came from the Amish, I was sure the prejudice I experienced would become even harsher. I did not want to face that. So I only glanced at John from afar, and I never looked him in the eyes.

The next year I went away to college and forgot about John.

As I listened to John I was acutely aware that I had done nothing to try to make it easier for him during high school. In order to fit in myself, I had been prejudicial toward someone in a position similar to my own. To feel good enough, I treated John as if he were invisible.

That is how prejudice perpetuates.

LATER LIFE

The years have gone by and my life has become more settled, resulting in more peace within myself.

Remembering My Father

On my bookshelf I see a picture of my father in his later years, warmly smiling, and I smile. Myriad memories flood through my thoughts.

I remember him shaking hands with me in his older years when I arrived or left his house.

I remember the softness in his eyes and the smile on his face as he held various infant grandchildren.

I remember every summer morning observing him slowly walking with his head bent forward, stopping now and then, examining each bloom in his rose garden. I knew there was a gentleness about him.

I remember the fragrance from the beautiful roses he grew.

I remember his rare but explosive anger early one summer morning when he discovered his young granddaughter had picked off all the buds from his rosebushes.

I recall the excitement in his eyes as he watched the black rose comb bantams he bought for me when I was a child. He liked them better than I did.

I remember one sunny summer day when he hired a driver to take him and me to a bantam show in a nearby town. At a food stand he requested a straw for me to drink my orange pop. He did not think it proper for women to drink straight from the bottle. I would have preferred tipping the bottle and taking a sip but was pleased that he saw me as a woman, even though I was only about eleven.

I remember walking home from school on a rainy day and watching in surprise as he passed me. However, he stopped to give the neighbor children a ride in his buggy. I didn't think it was right. Perhaps he picked them up because they had about twice as far to walk as I did. I didn't ask him about it because it was not acceptable to question my father's actions. I do know that treating his neighbors well was very important to him.

I remember that he almost never sent salesmen away without making a purchase. They knew he was a soft touch.

I remember him hesitatingly taking his first airplane ride at the age of eighty five. He went to Los Angeles with Alma to visit our sister, Ada. On the way back he sat next to an executive from MGM who gave him a business card and invited him to call on his next trip to California.

I remember being told by my sister Alma that my father stuttered badly in his youth. She said that was probably the reason he quit school in the sixth grade. My father told me that in his teenage years he read an article about a school in Indianapolis that helped people quit stuttering. He enrolled in the school and learned to speak clearly. He told me there were still several words that he couldn't say without stuttering, but he wouldn't tell me what they were!

I remember that my father did not follow all of the rules or expectations of the Amish church. Alma told me that as a young man he wanted to leave the Amish, but his parents were so strongly against it that he didn't. I believe he always regretted not having left. He was the seventh of twelve children. His three younger brothers joined the Mennonite church when they became of age. By that time my grandparents seemed to reluctantly accept their sons leaving the Amish.

I remember that my father had a sense of adventure and liked to experiment with unusual things. As a young man he bought one of the first Model T Fords in the county. At that time there was no rule in the Amish church against owning a car. Later, when the church forbade its members from having cars, he sold his. Whenever he spoke of that Ford, he had a gleam in his eye and a smile on his face.

I remember my father buying a large flock of sheep at a time when no one in the community had more than a few sheep, if any.

I remember that my father hired someone to bale his hay every year, in spite of church law forbidding it. And every year, in the middle of the day about a week before *ordnungsgma*, the church preparation Sunday before communion, we watched as a buggy with the bishop in it came rolling up our driveway. We knew that my father had once again gotten in trouble with the church and would have to apologize to the congregation for having broken the rule forbidding hay baling with a tractor. My brothers, sisters, and I assumed without question that he would continue baling hay with a tractor. He told the bishop, who was a friend of his, that it was easier confessing to the church than having loose hay in his barn.

I remember that my father secretly bought a car from a former hired hand who owned a Willy's dealership. He purchased it so my sisters, Ada and Fran could get to high school.

I remember when I was in grade school overhearing bits of conversation between my parents about possibly moving to Stuart's Draft, Virginia, in order to be a part of a more progressive church. My father wanted to go, but my mother adamantly refused, and we never went. Every time I drive along the highway in Virginia and see a sign for Stuart's Draft, I wonder how different my life would be if we had made that move.

I remember being told by Alma that my father was considered to be a very eligible bachelor in his day. He was handsome and owned a farm. However, he had great difficulty following through with commitment to marriage. He was engaged several times but always broke the engagement shortly before the wedding was to take place. Finally, at age thirty-three, he became engaged to my mother. She was from a well-respected family. Her mother had unexpectedly died when my mother was sixteen. Her father had just died from cancer. My father knew that if he ran this time, he would have the wrath of the community on his head. He got married, but it was hard for him at the beginning.

My father was a good man. My siblings and I got from him a love of nature, a sense of adventure, a desire to try new things, and a tendency to imagine the unusual. I can only guess that he must have been a man with internal conflict, feeling caught between what he wanted and the desires of his parents and the rules of the Amish church. He was curious. His yearning to experience new things did not fit with the church of which he was a part. My father wanted to leave the church but didn't feel he could without my mother joining him. However, he supported his children in going to high school and college, and their decision to leave the Amish. Eventually, because all her children left, my mother did agree with my father to join the conservative Mennonite church. Both of them seemed comfortable with that decision.

My father mellowed with age. His voice was softer. He greatly anticipated his children's visits. In the summer he delighted in our picking bouquets of beautiful flowers from his garden before heading home. Visiting him was a step back in time for me. I usually spent time with him on a Saturday. When I arrived in the summer he would always be sitting on the porch swing waiting for me. With a crinkled smile, he would laboriously push with both hands on the seat of the porch swing to help himself rise. As long as he was physically able, we went on an excursion, usually driving to Berlin or Walnut Creek for lunch. With a twinkle in his eye, he would gaze out the window at the flowers and trees as we traveled, enjoying the countryside. Often he saw someone he knew at the restaurant, and they would chat a bit. He would order custard pie for dessert, and I would ask for coconut cream or raspberry. We ate slowly.

My father and I sometimes stopped to visit a relative on the way home. After dropping him off at his house, I headed to my home in the city, traveling the one-and-a-half hour drive in silence, savoring my day. It was only when I neared my house that I turned on the radio to soft music, re-entering my world.

My father died in 1985 at the age of ninety-two.

Frivolous or Valuable

The degree of lively conversation during dinner surprised me. Adults fired their opinions back and forth about politics, religion, and whatever else was on their minds. People interrupted each other. The banter of two children was welcomed and respected. Chatter was boisterous.

It was the first time I had dinner with my future second husband at the home of Jewish friends of his. I was the only non-Jew present.

I enjoyed the conversation but seldom joined in. The banter back and forth was so fast. And it was so different from what I grew up with.

The messages I got from childhood were very clear. You didn't talk unless you had something important to say. Introversion was valued more than extroversion. You didn't interrupt someone who was talking. Mealtime was for eating, not for talking, and conversations at the dinner table were usually brief. Children were almost never considered to have anything significant to say when a group of adults was present.

Many major decisions were made when a person became a member of the Amish church. Most people didn't vote, so not much was said about politics. Religious issues were seldom discussed, because the rules and beliefs of the church were clear and had already been determined. Countless issues about life were decided by one's culture.

Conversation was usually direct, sparse, and unadorned. Common topics were the weather, illnesses of neighbors or relatives, neighborhood events, and the tasks to be done that day. It was considered frivolous to talk a great deal.

I remember my sister Ada being described as "the one who talks a lot" when she was a child. It was not a compliment. She probably was the kind of spirited, energetic child I hope my grandchildren will always be.

Of course there were many times within the family and between close friends when conversation flowed more easily.

I still tend to be quiet in groups, but less than in the past. I listen a lot. It seems necessary to have something important to say before opening my mouth.

I wish it were easier to let my thoughts and ideas flow.

I Married a Jewish Man

I married a Jewish man. Who would have thought that I would marry someone from a culture so different from my own? Sixty years ago when my husband and I were children, no one would have guessed that the little Jewish boy playing baseball in an empty lot near his Philadelphia row house and the little Amish girl roaming the fields on her Ohio farm would ever meet, let alone get married.

One day my husband said to me, "If our mothers could see us from heaven, my mother would say 'Oy vay,' and your mother would say 'Aye du yea.' But once they'd sat down and talked for a while, they would like each other."

Quilting with My Cousins

My cousin Mary invited me to a quilting in her home. I had never been to a quilting before; I awaited it with quiet anticipation.

Mary's house was built by her father, my uncle, on land which once belonged to a grandfather I never knew. I arrived there for the quilting at 10:15 a.m. on a Monday in the spring of 1994. Sitting in my car, I saw what once had been a familiar house and yard. They no longer seemed familiar. Every time I had visited this house previously, I had been accompanied by my sister or by one of my parents. Now thirty-some years had passed since I left the Amish, and I came alone. I felt shy, as if I didn't belong.

I was warmly greeted at the door and invited in. The women were already there, some having arrived as early as eight thirty a.m.

Twelve of us sat in a room with no electric lights around a large quilt in a frame. We were all cousins, aged forty to seventy.

We quilted. We reminisced. We talked about our lives and our children.

At 11:15 a.m. we were invited to the kitchen to eat lunch. Around a long table stood wooden chairs and a backless bench. I sat on the bench, as I used to at my parents' house when I was a little girl.

We quilted again. I asked my oldest cousin what my mother had been like when she was a young woman. At my question, quiet laughter rippled around the room, as if my query had prompted a new thought. I wondered if it had.

I looked up and saw two sisters sitting beside each other. They looked as if they could be twins, radiating a serene beauty enhanced by the simple lines of their white caps and dark dresses.

My cousins talked about tourists who invaded their world, stared, asked insensitive questions, and took pictures without asking.

The quilt became increasingly beautiful.

At 3:00 p.m. I said good-bye and drove home in solitude, savoring my day.

After an hour I neared my city world. I tuned the radio to soft music. As the melodies drifted around me, I understood with new certainty that my place in the city with my "English" husband was my world. And it felt good.

A Cultural Confusion

On a raw wintry evening, I was lying on the loveseat in our living room, my feet propped up, absorbed in a novel. Our two-and-a-half-year-old granddaughter, Madeleine, was quietly putting together a puzzle a few feet away.

Suddenly she stopped, jumped up, and bolted toward me, saying, "Please, Me'ma, I want soup."

I paused in my reading and told her I would get soup for her soon.

Madeleine was insistent, "Please, Me'ma, get me soup."

"Pretty soon, Maddie," I said and resumed reading.

She repeated, "Please, Me'ma, please."

Still engrossed in my reading, I muttered absent-mindedly, "You want soup, Madeleine?"

"Yes, I want soup, please."

I smiled at her and said, "I'll make soup for you."

As I followed her into the kitchen, she turned around, gave me a huge smile, and with a lilt in her voice, said, "Thank you for getting me soup."

As I prepared Madeleine's soup, I thought of earlier experiences I had with my stepchildren, David, Abby, and Jeremy, whose mother had carefully taught them to say please and thank you.

I was amazed and delighted that, as they readied themselves to leave the table after every evening meal, each would say, "Thank you for dinner."

I cannot remember ever even *thinking* of telling my mother thank you for a meal, no matter how delicious I thought it was.

One evening, when Abby, Jeremy, and David were teenagers, we sat at the dining room table laden with wonderful foods I had prepared—boiled red-skinned potatoes, roast chicken with dressing, gravy, green beans, and a garden salad. My specialty, a warm apple pie, was waiting in the kitchen.

I felt tired after a hard day's work but happy that I had prepared such a delicious meal for my husband and our family. All were present, except my son, Christopher, who was away at boarding school.

The children eagerly helped themselves to the abundance before them. Because I went to the kitchen to heat the rolls I had forgotten, I missed the passing of the food. When I returned, I asked Abby, "Will you pass the potatoes?"

She looked at me with fiery hazel eyes and asked, "What do you say?"

His face dark, David stared at me and said, "You are rude, Mary Kay."

Jeremy sat quietly with a smirk on his face.

I felt stunned and baffled. I had asked. I had used a pleasant tone of voice. I didn't demand. I said it the way I had always said it. No one else had ever even *implied* I was rude.

My stepchildren were incensed and repeatedly suggested I had bad manners. I pondered it for days, trying to make sense out of their indignation. One evening I translated, word for word, "Will you pass the potatoes, please?" from English into Pennsylvania Dutch, my childhood language.

And I realized there is no word for *please* in Pennsylvania Dutch.

In the culture I grew up in, if I spoke in a soft voice, asked rather than demanded, and treated others as well as I wanted to be treated, then I was considered polite. No special word was required.

Now, I try to remember to use the word please when I ask for something. And my stepchildren have grown up; they understand that politeness means more than using the right words at the right times.

Expanded Tastes

I love to go out to eat.

I drool as I remember the skewers of chicken dripping in peanut sauce served at a Chinese/Thai restaurant ten minutes from our home in Akron, Ohio; the cannelloni stuffed with ground lamb drowned in cream sauce from a small Italian restaurant in Zurich; the miniature chocolate-covered cream puffs with real pudding inside, served by a dancing, singing waiter at a restaurant near the train station in Florence.

I remember the most delicious meal I ever ate when my second husband, Larry, and I celebrated our fifth anniversary in a restaurant at the top of a hotel in Dallas. Herb-roasted potatoes and delicately flavored fish in cream sauce. I remember the huge globe artichokes and succulent mussels at an inn in Brittany, the tangy lemon soufflé offered at a two-star restaurant in Paris, the cream-colored crab cakes from Baltimore that I search for in other cities and never can find. The rich, dense, bittersweet chocolate mousse placed before Larry and me at a small restaurant in Cape May, New Jersey. I remember the ruhrecken and spaetzle, dribbled with gravy and served with warm fresh fruit in Switzerland.

It was all wonderful.

I did not always eat in restaurants.

I was astonished the first time I was invited to eat out. My brothers and I were attending Goshen College, and our sister Alma had stopped in for a visit.

"Let's go to the Pagoda Inn for dinner," Alma said to me and our brothers, Allen and Sam.

Her proposal amazed me. No one had ever before suggested that I go out to dinner simply for pleasure. Growing up Amish, the only time we ate a whole meal "out" was when we couldn't get home in time for the food my mother cooked. I remember eating hot dogs and French fries with my parents when we visited the Columbus Zoo. In high school, my friends and I would stop at the Dairy Queen. But eating out with my own family *for fun* was unheard of. It seemed an incredible waste of money. Reluctantly, I agreed to accompany Alma and my two brothers.

As we walked in the door of the Pagoda Inn, an Asian man wearing a black suit smiled, said good evening, and bowed slightly. The room seemed almost risqué with its intense red colors and dim light. Red chairs surrounded tables draped with white tablecloths. Asian designs were inscribed on red lamp shades, and silk fringe hung from the bottom of each. The high, lyrical sound of soft, instrumental music filled the air.

As the host seated us, a waitress appeared and handed us a large menu with a black cover. I looked inside and read the names of strange foods—spring roll, sweet and sour soup, Szechwan shrimp, Hunan chicken. I couldn't imagine what to order.

Alma looked intently at the menu and then at us. She smiled softly, and her eyes sparkled. With anticipation in her voice, she said, "The eggrolls are very good. Let's each get one. Oh, and the sweet and sour pork is delicious."

I had never eaten Chinese or any other foreign food before. Awkwardly, I tried to eat rice with chopsticks. We laughed as we kept dropping food on our plates. My brothers were older, had eaten with chopsticks before, and were more adept at using them. They did not drop their food as often as I did.

Alma looked at us with pride. She told us there were many other new foods and places waiting for us—rich sauces in Paris, scones and crumpets with tea in London, Wiener Schnitzel, bratwurst, and tortes in Germany, and chocolates in Switzerland. Alma was the oldest of my siblings and the first in my family to leave the Amish. She read a great deal. She was single and chose not to fulfill the traditional Amish expectation that young women should get married and raise children. Alma was also the first of both our immediate and extended families to go to college, and after graduating she repeatedly vacationed in Europe once or twice a year. To my sisters, brothers, and me, Alma was an example of what was possible.

But in spite of the excitement Alma exuded, I felt out of place at the Pagoda Inn.

I couldn't keep from thinking about the waste. All the money my sister spent and nothing to show for it. It was all gone, in our stomachs. And I could have eaten in the college cafeteria for nothing. Plus, I would have taken my mother's pan-fried chicken, mashed potatoes, and hot gravy any day over the food I was served.

I was not tempted to eat out again.

When I started to earn my own money after graduating from college, I occasionally brought home a pizza, ate a hot dog at a ball game, and picked up a cheeseburger and French fries at McDonald's. Several times I ate a steak at a restaurant. To buy food that was prepared for me was a luxury, a way of pampering myself.

All that changed in 1969 on my and my first husband's initial night in Zurich. We hungrily wandered the streets trying to decide where to eat dinner. We peered in the window of a small elegant restaurant with dark woodwork, soft lighting, and tables covered with white tablecloths. After checking the menu displayed outside the door and discovering that the exchange rate would allow us to eat well on a student's budget, we decided to enter. It was the beginning of often eating at restaurants with exquisitely flavored foods prepared in ways which were unknown to me.

My passion for food came into its own two years later. Along with my former husband and our four-month-old son, Christopher, I went on a week's vacation to an inn in Roscoff off the coast of Brittany in France. As we neared the town, we drove past fields of huge globe artichokes, an omen of things to come. Every meal we ate at the inn was an incredible adventure. Food was an art. I had never tasted artichokes with such a delicate flavor, each leaf dipped into a tangy lemon butter sauce. We were brought bowls of sweet mussels and slices of decadent chocolate tortes. The courses were served slowly, one after the other.

My love affair with food, which began in Roscoff, has intensified over the years. I have learned the delight and luxury of eating food prepared by creative chefs. I have learned to enjoy tasting flavors mixed together that I never thought of mixing, and ingredients combined that I never thought of combining. I am more adept at using chopsticks, and my husband, Larry, and I have eaten dumplings, noodles, and steamed fish in China, and kimchee in Korea.

Now if someone invites me out to eat, I will go in a second. And I do not doubt the pleasure I will receive from the money I spend.

Amish Bashing

It happened again. The dumb Amish stories. Faint smiles. Laughter. People shaking their heads in disbelief. One story tumbled after another.

I was eating lunch with six former teenage friends at Rosy's Family Restaurant. A few of the women I didn't remember having seen since I left high school forty years before. All were very nice women who helped their neighbors and attended church regularly. They wouldn't anymore think of not being in the church than they would of not eating. All had Amish neighbors. Most had "hauled Amish."

One told a story of a relative who was hired to drive Amish neighbors on errands. When she went to pick them up, the passengers included a goat that the Amish man wanted to take to a neighboring farm to be bred.

She protested. He insisted. And, of course, the goat relieved herself in the van. (Even I laughed.)

"But, no can mean no. And the car doesn't start if you don't turn the key. And the key is in your pocket," I thought to myself.

One of my former classmates stated that similar Amish seem to live in an area. In one particular region, the Amish are very sensitive and respectful, while in another, they are not very considerate.

With a smile in my eyes, I commented, "I guess the Amish are like everyone else. Some are kind and considerate. Others are not as sensitive to other people."

In the past, my friends from high school would never have told dumb Amish stories in my presence. Perhaps the passing of forty years, my mod haircut, black leather jacket, silver earrings, and Ph.D. nullified my Amish background in their eyes.

Throughout the years, I usually only heard Amish bashing when the storytellers either didn't know that I had been Amish or forgot. Or when I was sitting at the next table and overheard tales that weren't necessarily meant for my ears. In the past, the stories stung my whole body. The feeling behind the stories was like putrid smog that seeped into my impressionable high school and teenage experience. It echoed over and over, "You are not good enough."

It became such a normal penetration that I wasn't sure it was present until I was in communities where people didn't know I had ever been Amish. Then I was amazed at how differently I was treated. People initiated spending time with me, wanting to learn to know me.

Almost always the people who exuded the discriminatory feeling were religious. I believe it was because many of them had come from the Amish a generation or two earlier, and/or were often mistakenly identified by outsiders as being Amish and wanted to shed that perception in their own minds, as well as others'. For others, I believe Amish bashing has simply become a habit.

I was pleased that the stories that Sunday afternoon no longer pierced my spirit. I felt sad for the negativity that the stories spread in the world. I was sorrowful that the tale bearers, who were good women, had no inkling of the harm they were spreading. And I knew the stories were not about me.

Plain and Fancy

My hands are brown, wrinkled, weathered, and sprinkled with dark aging spots. Blue veins protrude, and my knuckles are bigger than they used to be. My thumbnails have a few more ridges, but polish covers those when I feel like putting it on. My fingers remain long and slender.

When I was a young woman, I had beautiful hands. They were handsomely tanned, smooth, and firm. They held no spots or noticeable veins. My hands seemed separate from my Amishness.

I remember sitting in a restaurant and glimpsing at the next table where women with wrinkled, weathered hands wore gorgeous jewelry. Emerald and sapphire rings. Gold and silver bracelets. Jewelry that was unknown to my mother's or my hands. Jewelry I couldn't afford.

I smiled as I knew that the expensive rings and bracelets on their non-Amish fingers and arms would look more comely on my young arms and hands. Even though I still felt Amish inside.

But the jewels belonged to them. And the young arms and hands belonged to me.

Today I have beautiful jewelry. My first ring was black onyx set in silver, which I purchased in honor of my first paycheck from my first real job. Since then, various people I love have given me jewelry. My sister Alma returned from Sauer's in Rio De Janeiro with a gorgeous petite necklace of four gemstones encased in gold. Several years later she lent it to me. I adored it. She eventually gifted me with it.

During one Christmas visit, my stepson's jewelry artist girlfriend presented me with a gorgeous silver pendant encasing a deep blue topaz. On my sixtieth birthday my husband handed me a royal blue velvet box holding sparkling diamond earrings. Several Christmases ago I discovered a Fed-Ex package on my doorstep from my sister Ada. It contained a beautiful black onyx choker necklace she designed and created. When my sister Alma died, I inherited a box full of jewelry.

One cold winter Saturday, I bought freshwater pearl earrings to add beauty to my life. Turquoise earrings from a trip to Arizona bring color to my wardrobe on a raw day.

In the morning when I am almost ready for work, my husband smiles as I try on first one piece of jewelry and then another, until I discover what fits for that day.

And I wear them on my weathered body with delight.

EPILOGUE

I gaze at the dancing flames and feel safe.

But will I continue to feel safe if I lay my stories out for the universe to see? I have no questions about having written them or about giving them to my son. Writing them has been like massaging balm into my soul. And my son is curious about where he came from.

I am not worried about the happy stories. People will enjoy those. But I am troubled about the painful ones.

There will be people who won't like my stories. They will say, "It didn't really happen that way."

I hear my mother's voice, "You don't talk about things if you can't say something nice," and my father's voice, "Bist du stolz?" (Are you proud?)

I hear my brother saying, "I wouldn't include that story," and one sister's, "I don't want my name or picture in your book. Nothing." (She later told me I could use her picture.)

And another sister, "Don't you take one thing out. That is the way it was, and people need to hear it."

I come from a culture whose very foundation is based on blending in. Publishing stories about oneself is not blending in. To purposefully stand out in a crowd is considered to be proud. And pride is not good.

For three or four years now, I have struggled. Do I dare print my stories? What will my life be like after I publish them? Am I brave enough to allow myself to hear and deal with the voices? Will I be able to have lunch at a restaurant in the small community where I grew up without being pointed out by people I don't know as "the one who wrote the book"? Is it arrogant to even think my book will be read? Will my high school friends still invite me to join them for lunch?

Might it not be much safer to write a novel and record the events I am trying to make sense of in my life as if they happened to someone else?

But writing a novel is not my way.

And if no one takes the risk and writes her or his reality, books would not be worth reading.

In the end, I am the one who has to decide, and I have decided. I have to speak my truth, knowing some people will disagree with my recollection of events, as well as disagree with my conclusions. I need to claim my truth as my own and let it fall where it may.

My intention is not to be hurtful to anyone, but to say how it was for me as a child, as a teenager, as a young woman, as a middle-aged woman, and as a woman with silver hair hobbling and dancing from one culture toward another, claiming and valuing parts of both.

My wish is that the sprouts that germinate from my stories result in healthy learning and dialogue. If so, publishing my writing will have been worth the risk.

My Family

I was born the youngest of eight living children to an Old Order Amish family in the 1940s. We lived on a farm in the largest Amish community in the world.

My father was a farmer, and my mother did the typical tasks of an Amish housewife: bearing and taking care of children, sewing clothing for the family, cooking, keeping a garden and house, and canning for the winter.

My oldest sister, Alma, started the migration to the non-Amish world. Not fitting the mold of the typical Amish young woman and tired of tending children and helping my mother keep house, Alma soon packed her suitcase and was ready to take off after she discovered my mother was once again pregnant, this time with her tenth child. My father promised that if she would stay and help until things had stabilized after the birth, he would pay for her to go to a Bible school of her choice. When the time came for her to leave, Alma chose a school in another state that had a high school and college. It also had a large library, which was a big draw for her because she loved to read. Eventually she graduated from college, taught a year of public school, and ended up as a newspaper reporter for a large metropolitan daily. She died in 1998.

As my siblings and I grew older, we all eventually left the Amish.

My oldest brother Leo's teacher visited my parents and asked that he be allowed to go to high school since he was unusually bright. My parents agreed he could go, but he would have to wear Amish clothes. He refused to attend high school with those restrictions. Later he took accounting classes by correspondence. He became a farmer with a prize herd of dairy cattle. Leo died in 1994.

My second oldest sister, Sarah, and my second oldest brother, Allen, did not attend high school either. Both took the high school equivalency test and went on to college. Sarah retired from a clerical position at a university. Her passion has been working on her house and yard, and recently, her condominium. Allen became a teacher and then a carpet layer. He died in 1980.

The last four of us went to high school.

My sister Fran became a teacher and married a man who became a Mennonite minister. She and her husband were church workers in Brazil for about thirteen years, then taught English in both China and Korea. Later they worked part of the year as support persons to Chinese scholars at a Mennonite university. They are now retired.

Ada completed one year at Goshen College in Indiana and several years later continued her education at the Fashion Institute of Technology in New York City. She lives in California and recently retired from Twentieth Century Fox.

Sam, the youngest of my brothers, became a physician. He is retired and spends a large portion of his time volunteering for his church. He helped found a hospice in his community and was its medical director for many years.

Because I was the youngest, I didn't have as many chores as my older siblings, and therefore had more time to roam the fields, read, and simply to be. I became an elementary school teacher, eventually earned a doctorate in counseling psychology, and am a practicing psychologist. I married a divinity student, had one child, divorced, and remarried eleven years later. My second husband is a family therapist.

After the Iraq war began, I felt it important to affiliate with organizations that dealt with conflict in a nonviolent way and became a member of a small progressive Mennonite church.

My sisters, brothers, and I all went to a one-room country school for the first eight grades.

At one time when I was living in Switzerland, my sister Fran was doing church work in Brazil, and my sister Ada lived in London.

SUMMARY
OF LESSONS

(OR SOME CONCLUDING THOUGHTS)

Most of the values my parents taught me have been very helpful in my life. Some I wish I had learned a little sooner and a little better.

My parents taught us strong values, and then generally trusted and supported us in following our passions, even when our desires were not what our parents would have chosen for us. As a parent I am aware how difficult this is to do.

Each of the cultures I have experienced has unique aspects that have provided tremendous richness to my life. I would like each of our children and grandchildren to have the experience of living in at least one other culture.

The impact of even chance encounters by acquaintances or strangers can have a huge effect on a person's life.

Fun and closeness within a family provides a catalyst that helps greatly in getting over the bumps in life.

Providing support to people going through a transition can ease the confusion in the process of making change.

Joining an organization as a newcomer and not following the traditions or rules usually results in stronger consequences than those same acts by a long time respected member of the organization.

Making a cultural change during the vulnerable adolescent and teenage years requires different skills than does making a transition when one is an established adult.

I cannot imagine any Amishman I know asking someone to transport a goat in her passenger van.

I would much rather that my granddaughters play musical instruments than become majorettes!

I am appreciative of all the lessons I have learned, and the wonderful people and experiences I have had in my life. I feel exceedingly rich.